ONLY BY
God's Grace
and DUCT TAPE

ONLY BY
God's Grace
and DUCT TAPE

Living Life in the Danger Zone

OPIE VOTIPKA

CITI OF
BOOKS

CITIOFBOOKS, INC.
3736 Eubank NE Suite A1
Albuquerque, NM 87111-3579
www.citiofbooks.com

Hotline:	1 (877) 389-2759
Fax:	1 (505) 930-7244

Ordering Information:

Quantity sales. Special discounts are available on quantity purchases by corporations, associations, and others. For details, contact the publisher at the address above.

Printed in the United States of America.

ISBN-13:	Softcover	979-8-89391-673-7
	eBook	979-8-89391-674-4

Library of Congress Control Number: 2025908991

Table of Contents

What do you remember most about growing up with 12 siblings?

There are two big things I remember most. First, I remember with awe how we all piled into one station wagon every Sunday morning to go to church. We always left at 8am to drive the 3 miles to church to be in our pew (2 nd row from the front) by 8:30 start. This was after the cows were milked, breakfast ate and everyone cleaned up and dressed.

Secondly, every morning and noon we all ate breakfast (oatmeal, toast, and orange juice) and lunch (either some kind of chicken or hamburger meal) together around a long folding table that we also used to play ping pong on.

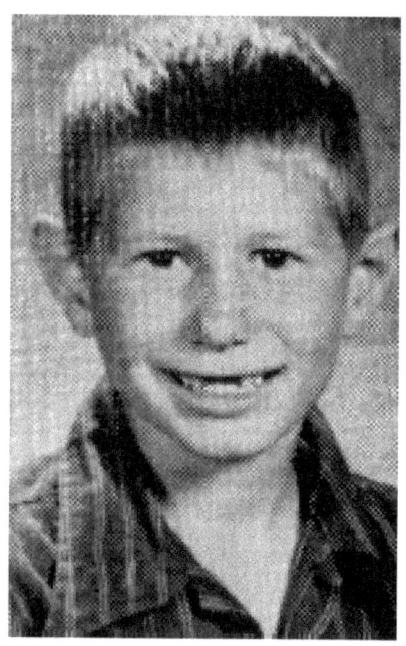

Pam wrote this article for a military magazine while we were stationed at Homestead AFB, FL

How did you figure out how to be a parent?

Wow! That is a tough question because most parents never feel that they ever truly learn how to be (good) parents. But before I answer this question I want to say that having grown up in a big family with lots of relatives, I alway knew that some day I wanted to have children and lots of grandkids. I saw how much my grand parents loved having their children and grand children around them.

Now to answer the question of figuring out how to be a parent. It was easy, I just followed the old adage: "Spank your kids 3 times a week whether they needed it or not." Just kidding!

First off, I believe too many people think you have to be prepared and be READY to have children. No one is ever ready so why not just jump into parenthood and roll with the punches.

In preparation for being a parent, I knew I needed to marry a "very beautiful" woman who not only wanted to have kids but was also good with kids. God graced me with Pam, and from our first real date I knew she exceeded those requirements and I felt confident she would make up for my poor parenting as I learned along the way.

As for figuring out parenting, I was blessed with godly parents and grandparents who set very good examples for me. I will admit that because my dad died when I was 16 I really struggled with how to be a good parent to the boys when they got to be young adults, I didn't have that example presented to me. I believe I just would try to give them every opportunity that I guess I wish I had been able to have had but didn't.

Trying to be the kind of parent I saw in my parents and watching Pam be a parent made being a parent easier until like I said the boys got to be young men. I tried my best to push them into the direction I thought they would enjoy (like I did) while at the same time trying to let them grow and make their own path and choices. I constantly told them to try it, as long as it is legal and moral. I wanted them to not fear risks and know that I was there to help them, but I probably pushed them off the risk cliff more times than I let them jump on their own (I fail at being patient).

I do believe I trusted God would help me learn to be a parent and would prevent me from doing too many dumb things. I also never wanted to be my children's friend, but their father that would help guide them and try to be a good example to them their whole lives.

So bottom line: I believe I haven't cornered the market on parenting and am still learning each day and with God's help, I will continue to learn more each day.

What responsibilities did you have on your family's farm growing up? What did you like the most? What did you like the least?

Over the years responsibilities increased as I got older. On a daily basis from a young age my responsibilities from getting out of bed to going back to bed were as follows:

1. Make my bed.

2. Get two gallons of fresh milk from the milk barn tank.

3. Help set up breakfast table.

4. Before I got ready for school, I cleaned out milk barn (scoopedout cow manure and washed and scrubbed the entire floor).

5. When I got home from school I prepared the milk barn for thecows (put grain feed and vitamins in each milking stall).

6. Go out to the cow pasture to bring the cows into the

milkhouse.

7. Help prepare the cows to milk by washing and cleaning theirudders and then helped milk the cows and pour the milk buckets in the milk cooler and took warm milk to feed young calves in the calves pen.

8. After cows were milked, I scooped the cow manure from thegutters and I prepared the milk barn for the cows for the next morning milking (Put grain feed and vitamins in each milking stall).

9. In the winter I put hay in the mangers of the cow barn forthem to eat during the night.

10. During the summer I helped with the baling of hay andpicking up and storing hay bales for use during the winter.

11. As I got older (10 years old) I was allowed to start drivingtractors and move them to different fields and at age 12, I actually got to use tractors doing field work (plowing and disking and cutting hay).

12. On Saturdays I helped hang clothes on the cloths line.

Now what did I like the most? Back then I liked getting the cows in the evening from the pastures because we had a minibike and got to jump hills and chase the cows around the pasture.

Now what did I like the least? Preparing the cows to milk in the evening because the flies were awful and every now and then got kicked by the cows. (I didn't mind cleaning up manure because I got a real sense of accomplishment from seeing a clean barn).

Christmas yard decorations. those aren't rock, just a plowed field.

Cynthia milking cows

Milk barn and Hay barn and Combine

Hauling bales

What was your Dad like?

As I had mentioned, my Dad went to be with the Lord early

January 1980, so 42 years ago when I was 16. I mention this before I answer the question of "What was my Dad like" because I will answer it in two different ways. The first answers will be what I knew of him from my birth to age 16 and the second answers will be what I have learned about him after his passing or after I was older than 16.

So what was he like? As I grew up I saw a very big, tough farmer who worked hard Monday through Friday and most Saterdays unless the Nebraska Cornhuskers were playing on Saturday afternoons. Sunday was God's day of rest and other than milking cows (which had to be done) we went to church and he allowed us to play the rest of the day with each other or cousins or neighbor kids. I remember a man who could bend metal with his hands to be welded onto some farm machinery, then turn around and be delicate enough to use a small needle to remove a sliver from my finger. I saw him wrestle large pigs and cows to the ground so they could be given medicine or be castrated so they would gain weight and he could have mountain oysters for breakfast. I saw a man who trusted his wife with all the finances but made the tough decision when they needed to be made.

Mom ran the household but my dad ran the farm and everything outside the house. As for being tough, I saw him numerous times because the only veterinarian in the county couldn't come to save a calf still in his mothers belly. My dad, without any large rubber gloves like the vet wore, was able to stick his hand and arm up to his shoulder inside the cow and wrap a cord around the calves feet so it could be pulled out because it was in the wrong position and couldn't be delivered head first. Paul Harvey's monologue "What is a Farmer" is spot on by the way.

My dad would get up at 4AM and start milking cows at 4:30AM and finish at 6AM, eat breakfast with his family, then his day would start by either taking a tractor to till the fields, or start working on repairing some equipment, or start building something needed by the animals. This would continue until noon when Mom would call everyone in for lunch. After lunch, especially during the summer afternoon heat, he would take an hour-long nap and then go back out to do something outside until we started milking cows at 4:30PM and finished at 6PM. He would then come in the house and clean up and eat supper while watching the "Joe Kennedy Weather report" on the local CBS station out of Lincoln. By the way Joe Kennedy was a WWII veteran like my dad, but fought in the Pacific and was a POW who had half his tongue cut off by the Japanese and had to relearn how to talk. After supper my Dad retreated to the living room and would watch 1 of the 3 channels on TV we had. He loved the Detective shows like: Cannon, Barnaby Jones, or Manix.

My dad was very Patriotic. He always made us stand when the National Anthem was being played, even on TV. He attended the monthly American Legion meetings and performed on the Honor Guard when a fellow veteran died or during Memorial Day celebrations.

My Dad loved having friends and relatives over and cooking out, especially 4th of July. He either purchased or allowed us to buy all sorts of dangerous fireworks. My dad enjoyed our birthday parties probably more than we did because he loved eating Angel Food cake and ice-cream (of which he would take his turn to hand crank).

As for sports he loved Nebraska Football and made sure we had sports equipment and good basketball backboard and net. He allowed us to play softball even though we pitched towards our big living room picture window and hit the ball towards the milk barn windows. He never played a game of basketball with me, but he did make some free throws to show he had played on his high-school team.

My Dad love God and showed it every Sunday by making sure everyone was clean and dressed and to church well before 8:30AM start time. Quite a feat for a family of 15. My Dad loved his wife and showed it by treating her like a queen and heaven forbid you ever sassed Mom and he found out about it or you would get a good spanking.

My Dad lived the Golden Rule. Many times he would go out of his way to help those less fortunate or needing help. I remember one time he came home with 6 sheep in the back of his truck and my Mom came out and said "Charlie, where did you get those sheep?" He said "Widow lady Michael". Mom said "You know we don't need any sheep", Dad replied "I know, but she needed the money." My Dad knew Mrs Marshal was too proud to accept his charity, so he bought sheep he didn't need.

Was my Dad a saint or perfect? No way! But he always tried to do the right thing for the right reason.

What did I learn about him when I got older? I learned he grew up very poor and had to hunt and fish to help put food on his family's table when he was young. I learned he loved his mother and took care of all her needs as she got older even while raising a large family himself.

He served as an Army medic in WWII, but didn't see combat until the D-Day invasion. He spent his first 18 months on the island of Bermuda doing autopsies on soldiers who died in North Africa from non-combat to determine their cause of death.

His friends he was drafted with that saw combat in North Africa never stopped giving him grief about his time in Bermuda.

I learned he was very smart and very practical and was highly respected by his friends and neighbors. He had the opportunity to go into any other careers but choose farming because he loved the challenge of it all. An example of his practical intelligence as the story goes: The day my dad and several of his friends who were drafted together and leaving on the train to Boot camp, all the friends showed up in their Sunday best clothes because they were being sent off by the whole town. My Dad showed up barefoot and wearing a raggedy pair of coveralls and his friends said to him "Charlie, we know you are poor, but you have better clothes than that." My Dad just shook his head and got on the train. The next day the train arrived at their Boot Camp and the Drill Sergeants yelled at everyone to get off the train and into the Reception building to get their Army gear. They all went through the line and started to put on their new Army fatigues and one of the friends asked the Drill Sergeant what they were supposed to do with their Sunday best clothes. The Drill Sergeant barked back at him and said "I don't care, mail them home if you want." Just as he said that all my Dad's friends looked and saw Charlie wadding up his old Coveralls and throwing it in the trash. They looked at each other and said, "That Charlie is the smartest guy we know."

My dad and his 4 sisters

My dad on the right as a medic in Germany somewhere

My parents with John

Hiedelburg bridge Germany

VOTIPKA FARM

Charlie Votipka happened to be home when he saw the storm approaching and loaded his 7 children in the car then sent for his wife and baby in the house and they drove to the celler ½ mile east on the old Charlie De-Long place. When down in the cellar, Fern said "Oh Charlie do we have all the kids?" They did have. Minutes later they return-ed to find only the house still standing. Their grade A Dairy barn and equipment gone. The combine had been carried out into his field and was a total loss The pickup and some other ma-chinery was also demolished.

Story of Tornado that hit the farm

My dad on the right in England waiting for D-Day

This picture says England 1945 but I believe it was in Bermuda in 1942 or 1943

My mom was 21 and my dad was about to turn 24

Mom and dad in Chicago before he left for England to prepare for D-Day Invasion

From Jim Kuhn: Your Dad is in the hat (#5) & Lillian is in the back (#9)

My dad in the middle and family

Nap after lunch

My dad on HS B-ball team

What was your Mom like?

My mother could be best described as a devout Catholic, a woman who love God with all her heart, mind, and soul. She was a devoted wife and mother, honored her mother and father, and was constantly working to take care of a busy household and help her husband manage a large farm and family.

Mom was very outgoing and like most DeWald women could talk all day long if you let them. Mom didn't know a stranger and loved to just sit and people watch when she traveled. Having been the oldest of 10 kids, she didn't seem to ever be afraid of doing anything or traveling.

She graduated High School as WWII was starting and moved to Washington DC from little old Alexandria, Nebraska to work in the US Department of Treasury. (Two of her uncles were FBI agents and one lived in the DC area). But not long after moving to DC, the Treasury Department moved to Chicago, IL. One of her aunts was now an officer in the Navy WAVES program. She also had an uncle who was a Navy officer, (All these aunts and uncles were her mother's younger brothers and sisters).

Mom loved to play cards and other board games with us kids, her husband, and her parents and brothers and sisters.

Mom loved to attend Mass and teach children's Sunday

school (52 years as a children's teacher). When we moved to Hebron after my dad passed away, she bought a house across the street from St Mary's Catholic Church and she attended early morning Mass every week day before she went to work as a cook in the only K-12 school in Hebron.

Mom enjoy baking bread and cooking for her large family. She also made sure we were always available to help our neighbors and her's and my dad's parents and families. He bread was renowned by everyone in the county and she gave it out as Christmas presents because people liked it so much.

Mom was known for helping others in need even if we were struggling financially also. When she wasn't taking care of her family she could be found at church cleaning and decorating, or picking up people who didn't have transportation to go to church.

Mom loved to sing at church, but she had a very high pitched voice and could be heard by everyone in church. She love Polka music and her CB Radio callsign was The Polka Queen.

She loved gardening and some years our garden was 3 acres in size. We were a self sufficient farm and pretty much the only reason she went to the grocery store once a month was because her sister Doris and her husband owned it.

Last but not least, Mom was the one who made quick decisions and my Dad was the one who took his time so they complimented each other as a husband and wife.

Bottom line, Mom was as Pro-life as you one can get. She loved people and tried to treat others as she wanted to be treated. I have most of her traits (especially the high squeaky voice). She didn't tolerated being sassed nor people or her kids that didn't want to work hard.

My mom in Chicago in 1942 on the steps of the Treasury department where she worked

My mom on those same steps 40 years later in 1982

Mom and Daddy with 2 of 13

My mom with younger siblings

My mother's parents (Ralph and Ferne)
Grandpa was know as RO DeWald (Ralph Oscar)

My mother and family her 11th grade year. probably 1940? Back row: Pat, Mom, Ralph, Ben, Doris, Phillip

Front row: Grandpa DeWald, David, Jane and Jean (twins), Mark. Grandma DeWald

Graduation Picture

Mom at age 2

The Fall before my father passed away.

That's me in mom's lap (1963).

Back row: Mary Jane, Kathy, John, Dan, Tom, Nancy

Front row: Cynthia, Mom and me, David, Daddy and Mark, JoAnne, Pauline

The Green house my Dad built for my Mom.

My parents in Chicago before my Dad went to England
to prepare for D-Day invasion.

Did your family ever go on trips when you were growing up? Where did you go?

I remember going on 5 trips as a family (never the whole family because a couple family members had to stay back to milk the cows).

First trip I remember was going to Oklahoma City (6 hours away) to attend my brother Tom's wedding in 1972. We left early in the morning, arrived at noon, wedding at 2, left at 5 to return back to the farm by Alexandria, NE 6 hours later. I believe we had 12 of us in a station wagon (no seat belts}.

Second trip I remember as a family was to leave after we milked the cows, we all loaded up and drove to Ashland, NE (1.5 hours away, near Omaha). My Dad's sister and husband rented a cabin on a small pond near Ashland and we went up there for the day to swim and eat lunch. We left in time to be home to milk the cows.

Third trip I remember was just me, a friend of mine, Mom and Dad and Rhonda took a 4 day trip to see several of my parent's friends they knew during WWII (my Dad from the Army, and Mom from the Department of Treasury). We didn't travel more than 2 hours a day.

We first went to Wichita, KS, then to a couple of towns on the way to Hays, KS.

Fourth trip was Mom, Rhonda and I in the summer of 1982 to go to my brother David's wedding in Myrtle Beach, SC. We first went to Chicago to see my Dad's sister Lillian and where my Mom lived and worked and attended church while she was working for the Treasury Department. Then we drove to my oldest brother John's house in Maryland. Then we drove to Columbia, SC to my sister Cynthia's home in Columbia, SC. Then we attended my brother David's wedding and then drove home. We were gone for a week.

The fifth trip was actually just before Christmas 1984 a couple weeks before I flew to Korea to be stationed there as an Attack Helicopter pilot for the Army. Mom and Rhonda and I drove to Alamogordo, NM to visit my brother David and his family. We were on the road for about 4 days.

So, bottom line taking vacations/trips were not something we really did much (kind of hard when you have lots of animals and kids). This is why if it wasn't for Pam, I would probably never go on trips or vacation because I never was shown an example of that.

What was your favorite animal on the farm? Did you name them or consider any of them pets?

————◆————

We had lots of dairy and beef cows, sheep, pigs, chickens, rabbits, cats and dogs.

The dogs were definitely pets and working dogs and we named them (Tramp, Barron, Gunner, Sandy). The cats never came in the house and we feed them with milk from the milk barn and they cats kept the mice and rat and snake populations down. We never named them other than calling them Calico cat, Orange cat, Tom cat, ...

Since none of the dogs were really mine, none were my favorite animals. My favorite animals were probably the pigs. Not really pets but we did call them Elmer Fudd, or Porky. I liked them best because they all became tasty bacon and great sausage. We enjoyed trying to hogtie them and wrestle them to the ground before we butchered them.

How did your family celebrate birthdays?

Birthdays were the same for everyone. My mom would make an Angel Food cake, no icing, put candles on it and light the candles. These birthday parties always happened after supper and after my Dad (who was always the last to come in from milking) got done eating.

We would get to have Angel Food cake and homemade ice cream and if we were lucky we could have a root beer float (for many years Mom made the root beer with sassafras roots).

You knew it was a special birthday if store bought root beer was used.

No presents were given (Christmas and 1st Communion only). And only family, no parties with friends.

My Dad and Mary Jane

My Dad and Kathy (when she returned from Vietnam) on my Dad's birthday

What was your favorite sport or game as a child? Did you have a favorite athlete?

$\diamond$

My Favorite sport was wrestling during High School.

Growing up we didn't have youth sports like today. We had enough brothers and sisters and cousins to field opposing football and basketball and softball teams. We didn't even know how to spell soccer let alone play it.

Even with just a few kids we would play football and baseball with just two of us. One would pitch and field, the other would hit and run bases. If you only made it to second base you would then go to bat and try to hit yourself in.

My brother Mark was the super sports enthusiast, I played whatever he wanted to play.

As for games: my favorite was Down on the Farm (Grandpa DeWald called it OH Hell, because that's what he would say if he lost a hand or even worse if someone played their hard wrong which caused him to lose). It was my favorite because we only got to play it at Grandpa and Grandma DeWald's house with them and Grandma always had a wonderful snack for us.

I enjoyed 10 Point Pitch and Acey Deucy which you could play with two people. I would play Dominos with my Mom sometimes also.

I really don't like watching professional sports (we rarely saw it on the only three TV stations we had). And the only college team was the Nebraska Cornhusker football team. I don't remember idolizing any of them. Mark loved all sports and probably could name you several players he liked. So basically I don't have a favorite athlete.

What was a typical day like for you when you were growing up?

I pretty much said it all earlier but I will put it all in orderly fashion.

Over the years responsibilities increased as I got older. On a daily basis from a young age my responsibilities from getting out of bed to going back to bed were as follows:

1. Make my bed

2. Get two gallons of fresh milk from the milk barn tank.

3. Help set up breakfast table.

4. Before I got ready for school I cleaned out milk barn (scoop outcow manure and washed and scrubbed the entire floor).

5. When I got home from School I prepared the milk barn for thecows (Put grain feed and vitamins in each milking stall).

6. Went out to the cow pasture to bring the cows into the milkhouse.

7. Helped prepare the cows to milk by washing and cleaning theirudders and then helped milk the cows and pour the milk buckets in the milk cooler and took warm milk to feed young calves in the calves pen.

8. After cows were milked I scooped the cow manure from thegutters and I prepared the milk barn for the cows for the next morning milking (Put grain feed and vitamins in each milking stall).

9. In the winter I put hay in the mangers of the cow barn forthem to eat during the night.

10. During the summer I helped with the baling of hay andpicking up and storing hay bales for use during the winter.

11. As I got older (10 years old) I was allowed to start drivingtractors move them to different fields and at age 12 actually got to use tractors doing field work (plowing and disking and cutting hay).

12. On Saturdays I helped hang clothes on the cloths line (we hadlots of cloths and the two cloths lines were 50' in length each).

There was never a lull in the day for there was always something that needed to be fixed or built, but from after lunch for at least an hour my dad always took a nap, so we kids would play softball or basketball or football during that break. Saturdays were very busy all day because Sunday we rarely did work (other than milking cows), Sunday was God's day of rest. On Sundays we either would go to our Aunt Pat's place to play with our cousins or we kids would go to play with the neighbors houses and play with those kids.

At night after dinner, Mark and I would play some sport in the yard until dark then come in watch what was on

TV until 9pm which was bed time until I was in High School. During HS football season we would attend the home football games, and basketball games at home also.

In High School we were allowed to go out for one sport. During that season we were allowed to miss milking and supper to go to away games.

Butchering 500 chickens during the summer

Wintertime behind the milk barn.

Cynthia setting up the milking machine.

Hauling bales. This would have been the trailer I fell off of and run over by trailer tire.

Who was your closest friend growing up?

My closet friend growing up can be split up into 3 different age categories.

But first of all I will say that because we lived on a farm that even though Mark was my brother, he was pretty much my "Friend" I did everything with most of my years birth-10th grade.

But K-4th grade I would say my closet friend other than Mark was a kid name Kevin Wolf. He lived in Alexandria and his dad was an Insurance agent. We road the bus to school together and played together during school. I never saw him outside of school because we didn't live near each other and on weekends we worked on the farm and on Sunday he went to the Methodist Church and I went to the Catholic Church.

4th-10th grade I changed school districts from the local Meridian Schools to Hebron Schools. I became friends with a kid named Dennis Hinze. He was also from a farm outside of Hebron so we were both kind of outcasts (sort of because we didn't attend K-4 with the other kids). Dennis liked to play war games when we were younger. As we got in middle/early High School we both started to get into Hotrod cars. Difference was he was an only child so his parents could afford pay for him to fix up and paint a hotrod car. We were in the band and Marching band together. He play trumpet and I played the French Horn. For sports Dennis played basketball and I wrestled (neither of us were good enough to play varsity).

From 6th-10th grade my brother-in-law Roger Retzlaff's nephew Jeff came to live with us to get him out of the big Lincoln schools that were not a good influence on him. So I can say Jeff was a close friend but he and Mark had more in common (like working a cars). As the years went by Mark and Jeff were closer friends. But we all three played softball, basketball, and football together on the farm. We also were able to buy some used motorcycles so we road them around together in the fields. We also hunted pheasant and quail in the winter together. Jeff moved back to Lincoln when we moved to Hebron after my Dad passed away and Mark went into the Army the summer after he graduated and finished my 10th grade year.

10th-12th Grade years we moved to Hebron and I got more into sports and higher level academic classes and Dennis got more into cars and girls so we didn't pal around much together. But I started to became good friends with Greg Bodtke to play basketball and were in some classes together. Gregs parents owned and ran one of the grocery stores and Greg lived a few blocks from me. I have maintained my friendship with Greg all these years and he has traveled to see me several times and was a groomsman in my wedding and I in his.

So other than my brother Mark, Greg I can say has been my closest friend growing up. Dennis I have seen on a few occasions and Kevin I don't believe I ever saw again once I moved school districts (in July 2023 when I was in Alexandria, NE for out family reunion and was staying with my aunt Doris DeWald, she took me on a tour of Alexandria and informed me that Kevin fixes all her small equipment and now lives in the house he grew up in down the road from Aunt Doris).

How did you get your first job?

Depends on what you mean by my first job. Do you mean Paid or Unpaid?

If "unpaid" I would have to say taking care of the animals on the farm and driving tractors in the field and cutting and hauling bales. Now Mark and I would get paid 50cents helping my Grandpa DeWald cutting thistles in his fields.

If "paid" I would have to say working for a big farm 20 miles north for a few weeks de-tassling hybrid corn. My cousin Tracy DeWald and his sister recruited Mark, Me and Jeff Retzlaff to work a few weeks helping out. They got paid a bonus for recruiting us.

During my summer between my 11th and 12th grade years I worked for a farmer part-time helping him spray weeds and moving irrigation pipes. This farmer's daughter was friends with my sister Rhonda and told her he needed some help.

But my first non-farm job was running the projector at the Hebron movie theater and putting up the words on the outdoor display. They only played movies on certain nights so it was really a part-time job and that allowed me to be on the cross-country team and wresting team and track team my 12th grade year. I got the job because one of my teacher's wives managed the theater and he asked our class if anyone would be interested in the job. I didn't get paid much but got free popcorn and got to go to see the movies for free. I remember running the projector for R-rated movies and I wasn't of age to attend the few movies I ran of the projectors for. When I graduated I got my cousin Steve Hergott the job.

What did you do in the Army?

Forty-one years ago this last January I signed my Enlistment into the US Army as a 67T (UH-60 Blackhawk) Tactical Helicopter Mechanic. Since the Blackhawk was just being fielded the soonest class date for training I could get was September 1982. But 42 years ago in the summer of 1981 I started the process to apply for the Army's Warrant Officer Flight Training program (WOFT). The majority of Army pilots are Warrant Officers and they are not required to have bachelors degrees.

You might be asking why did I want to be a pilot or to join the Army? My brother David had graduated from the Air Force Academy in 1980 and a year later was graduating from Air Force pilot training in Del Rio, TX. My sister JoAnne had spent 3 years Active duty in the Army as a helicopter mechanic and was applying for WOFT with the Colorado National Guard where she was serving part-time as a UH-1 mechanic and attending Colorado Aero Tech getting her Airframe and Power Plant license. Two of my brothers-in-law, Roger Retzlaff and Byron Bond, had served as Infantrymen in Vietnam and told me about the Army Warrant Officer pilots that flew them into and out of combat zones. Having heard my family members talk about military exploits and flying and watching many war movies plus seeing military and civilian airplanes and helicopters flying over our farm I decided I wanted to be a pilot even though I had only flow once in a small airplane. Also, I knew that to be an Air Force pilot I would have to get a bachelors degree and I knew that with my less than sterling HS grades I would probably have a hard time to get into college (back then less than 20% of students went to college right out of HS). But I had scored very high on the Military entrance test (ASBAB) and the Army Flight Aptitude Selective Test (A-FAST) and there wasn't a requirement for a Bachelors. Also my HS Auto mechanic teacher, Mr Goodrich, was a 22 year Air Force mechanic and was mentoring me and an other classmate Tim Sterba about being aircraft mechanics and if we worked hard, to become Air Force pilots (more on that later).

As a rising HS senior my original plan was to join the Army, go to WOFT, do 4 years as a helicopter pilot and return to Nebraska to fly helicopters and fixed wing crop dusters. I had no intention of making a career of the military, but God had other plans and orchestrated the rest of my life in ways I couldn't foresee. But as I look back, God's plan was much better than mine and made me a much better pilot and military officer and person in general.

So as I started the process to apply for Army WOFT, my recruiter made me promise that if I didn't get accepted into WOFT that I would enlist into the Army as a helicopter mechanic. He told me that the WOFT application process was long and laborious for him and he would appreciate getting an enlistment towards his annual recruitment goal. He also said (and JoAnne verified) that the majority of WOFT students were already enlisted in the Army and the majority of those were mechanics. What he and JoAnne didn't know was that pretty much all Civilian direct of WOFT had at least an Associates degree and a private fixed-wing pilot license (neither of which I had). The process was lengthy because I had to take an in-depth flight physical and interview before a small board of recruiting officers. Then my paperwork went before a review board that only met quarterly, so my paperwork didn't meet the board until December 1981. In mid January 1982 I was informed I selected by the board as and Alternate for WOFT, to which my recruiter said he had no idea what that meant as far as actually getting a Primary slot. He recommended I go ahead and enlist for 67T slot and if my WOFT application moved from Alternate to Primary slot I could revert to that at that time, but enlisting in immediately I would guarantee my 67T training. So on 26 January 1982 I enlisted in the Army with a Basic Training start date of 10 September 1982 at Ft Jackson, SC with UH-60 mechanic training set for 1 December 1982 at Ft Eustis, VA. (a few years later I found out that my recruiter was wrong and that once I enlisted for that 67T position I was taking off the Standby list for WOFT and if I had stayed on the Standby list I probably would have go to Basic Training the about same time in September and then to WOFT versus 67T training. But as I will explain later, God was in control and it proved to be the better move to enlist in)

In September 1982 I was bused to Ft Jackson, SC (my sister Cynthia and her husband Rick worked on Ft Jackson at the time so I got to see them every Sunday afternoon). Basic training was 8 weeks of learning how to be an Army soldier, qualifying expert with an M-16 and all the other training that is mandatory back then. I was actually in very good physical shape so instead of losing 10-15 pounds like most of the guys I actually gained 5 pounds from all the pushups I had to do.

I finished Basic Training the day before Thanksgiving with sister Cynthia and brother David's families at the graduation and got to spend Thanks Giving day and the weekend at Cynthia house. I boarded a bus and went to Ft Eustis, VA to start my 67T UH-60 Tactical Helicopter training. Mechanic training was 3 months long and having worked on cars and trucks growing up it was a breeze. The only new thing I learned was how to use Safety wire on the all the bolts. Since the Blackhawk was new and the majority of them going to Ft Campbell, KY our of our class of 13 of us were going to have to go there and only 2 slot were available for Ft Lewis, WA (my sister Nancy and her family lived 2 hours from Ft Lewis so I wanted to go there). Only myself and one of the two Sergeants (they were retraining to 67T) wanted to go to Ft Lewis. So guess what the Army did? The sergeant (E-5) and another private E-1 who didn't want Ft Lewis (I was also an E-1) got the Ft Lewis assignments. This was my introduction into how the Army rarely looks at your "Dream Sheet" (Assignment request form). Looking back I can see how Satan had his hands in that decision to send me to Ft Campbell (more on that later). The other guy who got Ft Lewis and I were both E-1s so the local Personnel office let us trade base assignments (I did have to bribe the other E-1 $150 to make the trade). While I was finishing up at Ft Eustis I decided to update my WOFT package with a new Flight Physical and actually tried to reapply for the WOFT program there at Ft Eustis but the Sergeant at the Personnel office recommended that I wait until I arrived at Ft Lewis in a month. The Sergeant said that if I submitted the application at Ft Eustis it would be much harder for me to keep track of its progress and that if it go lost in the process I would have a hard time figuring out where from 3000 miles away. So I waited.

We finished training and and I was off to Ft Lewis via a short stop in Nebraska to see my family. I flew into Seattle and took the bus down to Ft Lewis and in-processed to the 9th Infantry Division. I was assigned to C Company 9th Combat Aviation Battalion. C Company had just switched from the old UH-1 Hueys to the new UH-60 Blackhawks the month prior so was in need of mechanics and Crewchiefs. Crewchiefs were mechanics who flew on the missions and provided mechanic support and doubled as Door Gunners when we carried M-60D machineguns. My first day at C Company I had my initial meeting with my company commander and after briefing me on his expectations he asked if there was anything he could do for me. I said I would like to apply for WOFT and needed his signature and not knowing I had my application updated and with me he said "Sure, when you get it all together bring it to me and I'll sign it." The look on his face was priceless when I pulled out my application out of my briefcase and said "Well sir, I actually have it right here ready to be signed." Without missing a beat, he took it from me and signed it and said "Very good, now take it over to the Battalion Commander across the street for his signature." I walked across the street and met the Battalion Commander's secretary and she set up an appointment for a week from that day. During that week I in-processed in C Company and was issued my tool kit and met all the other mechanics, two of which who were Sergeants and had applications in for WOFT and were waiting for class dates for the last 9 months. During that week I was evaluated on my ability to work alone on different aircraft and passed my evaluation. My Battalion Commander meeting time arrived and he sat me down in his office to interview me and look at my test scores. After about an hour he said "you have very good test scores and did well in Basic Training, but you have only been in the Army for less than 6 months and don't have any awards or promotions (he was comparing me to the Sergeants in the unit). But I'll sign your package anyway and you need to take it to the Brigade Commander for his signature. So I drove the mile to the Brigade HQ and gave my application to the Commander's secretary and she said I'll call you when to come back. Since it took a week to meet with the Battalion Commander I figured it would take a month to get an interview with the Brigade Commander. The next day the Brigade secretary called and said "come pick up your application the Brigade Commander signed it." I said "I don't need an interview", she said "No, just come get it and take it to the Division personnel office." So I did, I took my application to the Division personnel office and they took it and said it would be sent to Decision board meeting the next month. (Two years later I was in Korea flying AH-1F Cobras and was tasked to go fly General Harvey on a tour of the DMZ, two years before he was Colonel Harvey and was the Brigade Commander who signed my application without interviewing me. When he got in the front cockpit I jokingly told him that if anything went wrong it was his fault because he was the final say on my application. He laughed and we flew around for about an hour and I took him back and he thanked me for not making him regret his decision to sign my application. Then he laughed and went on his way.)

So during the next month I was designated a Crewchief and assigned my own UH-60 to maintain. I was promoted to E-3 six months early because they didn't want E-2s in charge of aircraft. It was a $100 per month raise, so now I was making $525 per month (I was living in a dorm and eating in a dining facility for for free. I sent home $250 per month to help my mom and I had a $100 per month car payment. That $225 left over was more money than I knew what to do with so I started to take night college classes on the base). During that month I began to fly on troop carrier missions and got checked out using Night Vision Goggles which were just starting to be used in helicopter units.

After about a month, I received a call from the Division personnel office and was informed I had received a

Board score of 245 out of 300. I ask what that meant and they said it was very good. I asked the two Sergeants in the unit what their Board scores were and one said 201 and the other 199. (I later found out that what the Army did was rack and stack application based on Board scores and since mine was higher I was put in a higher priority for actual WOFT training even above guys who had submitted a year before). So during that summer and as fall approached I continued to go to night school, fly on missions day and night, and decided to join the Ft Lewis parachute club where I made two static line parachute jumps from an Army UH-1 Huey. During the past year my sister JoAnne had been at WOFT at Ft Rucker, AL and was graduating around 1 October 1983. My mom and other siblings were in attendance at her graduation but I was still at Ft Lewis, and the morning of her graduation I received a call from Division Personnel that I had to giving a WOFT training date and had to report to Ft Rucker in 10 days. I asked how many days I was permitted to drive to Ft Rucker and they said "8", then I asked how many days does it take to out process from Ft Lewis and they said probably 5 days and that I had better get out-processing. I called JoAnne at Ft Rucker and congratulated her and told her I would buy her car and she could ride to Nebraska with our mom because I was coming there in 10 days. I ran and told my immediate boss and drove to Division personnel to get all the paperwork I needed to out-process and travel to Ft Rucker. I raced through out-processing in 2 days (Since I had only been there 6 months I didn't need as much to get signed and I forged a couple of Initials to places I hadn't ever been to). The whole battalion was in total shock as I was the first to go to WOFT ahead of guys who had be in the unit for 2-3 years. I gave my car keys to Sgt Steve Bedding (he was the one with the 199 Board score) to sell my car after he dropped me off at the Seattle airport to fly to Nebraska to personally congratulate JoAnne and then to Columbia, SC to see Cynthia and Pauline and their families (Pauline was there finishing her PA training at Ft Jackson). With one day to go I boarded a Greyhound bus to Ft Rucker and signed in to start my Army pilot training.

I had recently turned 20 and was assigned to Class 84-11 Purple Flight with a group of guys ranging from 20-36 years old (the vast majority were 26-30 and had several years of military experience). I soon found out that 6 of us were from Ft Lewis, 8 from Ft Campbell, and other 12 were from various bases. Half of us were helicopter mechanics and the the other half were Infantry, Ranger, Tankers, and Military Policemen. (Hal Hughes was 36 and came from Ft Lewis also). During the next couple weeks we prepared for the Officer training portion called Warrant Officer Candidate Development (WOC-D) and were "Volun-told" to do community service by working at a local Halloween Haunted house that was raising money for a local charity during the last to weeks of nights that October. November 1st we started 4 weeks of WOC-D, kind of like Basic Training but we didn't carry weapons and was more about learning how to be an Officer. Because of Thanksgiving we ended up finishing right before Christmas break and I spent the next 2 weeks at my sister Cynthia's for Christmas.

The first week of January 1984 we started Primary Pilot training where we learned to fly the little TH-55. From learning how to hover to making Emergency engine failure autorotations, this training lasted 3 months. All the while we had to keep our barracks in Inspection shape and even the married students had to earn the privilege to leave the barracks on the weekends. After we mastered the TH-55 we moved on to UH-1 Contact where we learned to fly the iconic Vietnam era Huey so we could later fly the aircraft in Instrument training. UH-1 Contact lasted 4 weeks and we moved on to Instrument training where we spent 3 weeks flying both the aircraft and full motion simulators. Our class was split into two sections where half did their training during the day and the other half at night. Roger Omenhiser and myself were put on the night schedule with a good portion of the 2nd Lieutenants that us WOCs were aligned with. After we passed our Instrument flight training we were "racked and stacked" as to our class performance and ranked 1-24 and got to pick our track of either Lift aircraft (CH-47 Chinook, UH-60 Blackhawk, or UH-1 Huey) or Tactical aircraft (AH-1 Cobra or OH-58 Kiowa).

We had 1 CH-47 Chinook, 4 UH-60 Blackhawks, 6 AH-1 Cobras, 4 UH-1 Hueys, and the rest would be given Oh-58 Kiowas. All the other aircraft mechanics in my class selected the kind of aircraft they had worked on. Kermit Upshaw was Number 1 in the class and had been a Navy scuba diver and he picked a Blackhawk. I was the Number 2 student in my class and everyone expected that since I was a Blackhawk mechanic I would pick a Blackhawk also, but I didn't, I picked the 1st Cobra slot (I will explain later how God blessed that decision). The guys who picked Lift aircraft continued to fly and train in the UH-1 where those of us who pick Tactical aircraft transitioned to the OH-58 for Aeroscout training for the next 5 months. We learned how to fly it in a tactical environment and learned how scout for enemy targets and navigate while flying at tree top level both day, night and with Night Vision Goggles (NVGs). During our last couple months in training we submitted our dream sheet for our follow on assignment after graduation. I was told flying in Korea would allow me to gain more experience faster and that anyone who put Korea as a choice got it. So I only put Korea down as a choice. Of us 6 future Cobra guys, I got Korea, Roger Omenhiser, Mike Blair, and Jeff Smith got Germany, and two guys named Doug Brown both got Ft Hood (one of the Browns was one of the first AH-64 Apache pilots). Graduation was

20 September 1984 and I started Cobra training a month later and completed it right before Christmas with a report date of 4 January 1985 for Korea.

On my way to Korea I stopped and spent 3 days in Hawaii with my cousin Rita Hergott and then off to Seoul Korea. Before I left Ft Rucker all the instructors told me to try to get assigned to D Troop 4th Squadron 7th Cavalry Regiment (D 4/7 Air CAV Squadron) because they were located away from all the Infantry unit by themselves. I thought how is a brand new WO1 going to make that happen? (But God could). Two sister Air CAV Troops were located 10 miles away the base with two large Infantry Brigades so the aviators were outnumbered 10-1 and were second class citizens on that base. I spent a few day in Yung Song Army Base in Seoul and by God's Grace I was assigned to D 4/7 CAV at Camp LaGuardia, located in the middle of Uijeongbu City (sounds like: We-jon-bo City). The original MASH 4077 the Movie/ TV show M.A.S.H was based on was on the north side of Uijeongbu and when we took off to the north we could see the helicopter landing area that was still there 30 years later. The Air Cavalry mission was to scout for the enemy and help the ground troops know the best attack position. We also patrolled the Demilitarized Zone (DMZ) between North and South Korea just letting the North know we were watching. We had 7 AH-1 Cobras, 10 OH-58 Kiowa, 3 UH-60 Blackhawks, 1 UH-1 Huey, and a Platoon of Infantry Scouts. It was a great first assignment because we had to progress in our training quicker than my counterparts in the States and Germany because everyone was on 1 year rotation whereas the other unit's pilots were there 3-4 years without a lot of turnover. All our senior Cobra pilots/ Instructors had all seen combat in Vietnam and were expecting us to be ready for the North Korean hoards that could attach at any minute. We were located within North Korean artillery range and were on alert status

7 days a week. Our running joke was "Thank Goodness It's Friday, only 2 more working days until Monday." The flying was very good and the I became a full up Pilot In Command (PIC) Day and NVG within 6 months as opposed to 2 years in the States. During my off time I walk the mile to the next bigger Army compound and took College Level Examination Program (CLEP) and Dauntes tests towards my Bachelors degree. I passed all 5 basic CLEP tests and several Dauntes tests and would end up receiving 36 college hour credit from Embry-Riddle Aeronautical University (ERAU) a couple years down the road because of these tests (kind of like taking AP tests). I also took part in a play production of "The Odd Couple" where I had a small part but I was able to get UH-60 transport from my Squadron to the different outposts we performed at versus having to take vehicles. As September rolled around I, like the other single guys, submitted my request for a 6-month extension in Korea with follow on of Ft Bragg, NC. A month later I received word my extension request was denied but my assignment to Ft Bragg was approved with a report date of 4 January 1986. Everyone was shocked that a single guy's extension request would be denied. I was told to call Department of the Army Warrant Officer Assignments to ask why. The next day I called and the Assignment's manager told me I was needed at Ft Bragg, but if I wanted to receive and extension I would have to accept an assignment to Ft Hood, TX. I didn't like that idea so I said "I'll be at Ft Bragg on 4 January." in November since I hadn't taken any leave so far that year I was given the opportunity to fly on an Air Force C-130 to Chigido Island on the south shore of South Korea and spend week over Thanksgiving there. The USO had a small complex on this "Vacation Island" where we were allowed to hunt Pheasants and learn how to mountain climb and repel. I returned to Camp LaGuardia and started to prepare for my departure.

I finished out my tour of Korea on 19 December and flew back to Nebraska to see family and then flew to Columbia, SC and borrowed a car from Cynthia (I had a car before I went to Korea and let Rhonda use it in college but back in October 1985 a drunk driver destroyed it in the middle of night while it was parked outside her house). Before I left Korea I was told to get into D Company 82nd Aviation Battalion. D Company was an Attack Helicopter unit as oppose to an Air Cavalry unit (Ft Bragg had 1/17 Air CAV Squadron also). Attack Battalions waited until the Air CAV found the enemy tanks and then would fly en mass to attack them. Same AH-1 Cobras but Attack units carried more Anti-Tank missiles and less fuel because we would spend much time airborne where the Air CAV Cobras carried more fuel and less missile so they could spend much more time airborne looking for the enemy. Ft Bragg is the home of the 82nd Airborne and I was issued a maroon beret to wear verses a BDU cap. The Beret was an esprit-de-corps thing that separated the hard charging Airborne Paratroopers from the low life "leg" Infantry. Well, by God's Will I was assigned to what would soon become B Company, 82nd Attack Helicopter Battalion (my new commander of B Company married Pam's best friend Ginger a few years later). I quickly jumped into my duties and because of my NVG experience started training all the new guys and started night college courses at the ERAU-International Campus located on Ft Bragg. Semesters were actually done in 8 week periods. Once I would have 4 classes a week (2 on Monday and Wednesday 5-7pm and 7:30-9:30pm and 2 classes Tuesday-Thursday 5-7pm and 7:30-9:30pm). But normally because of my work schedule I would only be able to take 2 classes per 8 week period and I did one 8 week period of Saturdays for 8 hours each Saturday. Because ERAU awarded me 45 credits for being a Pilot, 36 credits for my CLEP, 6 credits for the Warrant Officer Advance course by Correspondence I only need 13 classes

(39 Credit hours). Since ERAU required that I take at least 30 credit hours with them this worked out perfectly. I figured I could finish my degree by December of 1986, but I ended up having to miss an 8 week period to attend Army Airborne training at Ft Benning, GA for 3 weeks. This worked out perfectly, because after 8 months of full-time work and going to night school I had time to go see my cousin Joe DeWald who was stationed at Cherry Point Marine Corps Air Station. What I didn't expect was that I would meet the most beautiful and smart southern belle at Atlantic Beach on my return from trying to see my cousin Joe DeWald at Cherry Point. My life was changed forever in that fateful evening that was the equivalent of 2 meteorites crossing paths at night. I had an 8am mission I had to fly the next morning and I still had 2 hours of driving to get home and she had come to Atlantic Beach against her will with her friend Ginger. But God's timing is perfect!!!! We only talked for 20-30 minutes and going against her better judgement she gave me her phone number (I am sure there have been days she has regretted doing that. Haha).

During my first year and a half at Ft Bragg I flew a lot of training missions and exercises both day and night both in the North Carolina and other military bases in Georgia and California with the Attack company. I also attended and graduated Army Airborne training, married the love of my life, and finished my Bachelors Degree. During this time it was announced that our Attack Battalion was going to transition from AH-1s to the new AH-64 Apache and I chose to not accept that transition and was scheduled to switch to the 1/17 Air Cavalry Squadron on the other side of airfield for my last year at Ft Bragg. Once I moved to the 1/17 Air Cavalry we were constantly on the go because now since the 82nd Attack Battalion had shut down for a year for its transition to the AH-64 we were the only large AH-1s on the East Coast to support a lot of operations. We deployed to Ft Chaffee,

AR, Ft Drum, NY, Camp LeJeune, NC, Honduras, and almost deployed to Kuwait during the Iraq/Iran war to

AH-1F Cobra

The photo of me with a Parachute was actually when I was in the Air Force as an ALO/FAC in Sept 1994 before we boarded our C-130 to make a night Combat jump into Haiti for Operation Just Kidding (actually Operation Just Cause, but since we ended up not jumping we changed the name). The helicopters are AH-1F Cobras like I flew and one is me in the cockpit. The Tilt rotor plane on the bottom was the XV-15. I saw it fly into and Land at Ft Rucker and believed I would get to fly it one day. 2 years later the program was cancelled, but was revived 25 years later to become the Marine Corps and Air Force V-22 Osprey used today.

This was one of the two original XV-15s that flew into Fr Rucker when I was in WOFT. I thought I was going to get a chance to fly it one day.

My First civilian parachute jump at Ft Lewis, WA

The Purple ball cap is what we wore in WOFT to color code each class for easy identification. The mug was our class motto: 84-11 Cold Steel Knight Flight

Wedding day

Mom pinning on my WO-1 bars

Sgt Biddinger, one of the other senior UH-60 Mechanics at Ft Lewis

The mighty TH-55 we first learned to fly in.

An OH-58A we flew for Aero Scout training my last 4 months at WOFT.

My solo certificate in the TH-55.

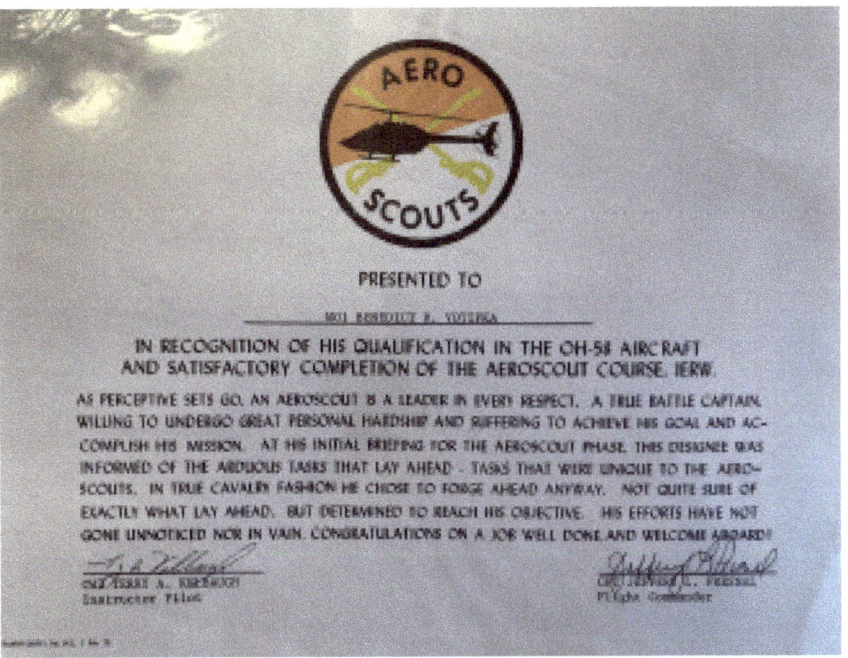

Certificate from Aero Scout training

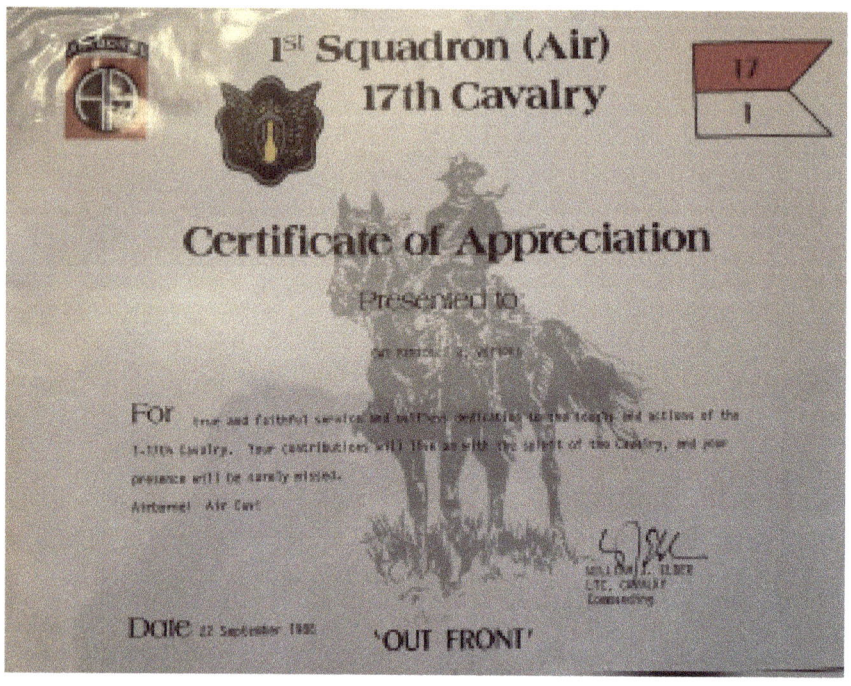

Me in Korea at Camp LaGuardia

Me in the Field for an exercise at Ft Bragg Range

My mother and sisters visiting at Ft Bragg after Pam and I got engaged (I believe around Thanksgiving)

JT when he came to visit.

Flying through Washington DC on our way to Ft Drum, NY

On out way back from Ft Drum, NY

Me at a Kick Boxing contest in Korea

Shooting Russian AK-47s at the Ft Bragg Range.

What were all the places you lived in when you were in the Army?

In the last section about what I did in the Army I mentioned all the major places I was stationed. Now I will put down a list of places and dates where I was stationed or went for a training exercise.

Sept-Nov 1982: Ft Jackson, SC. Basic Training

Nov 1982-Mar 1983: Ft Eustis, VA. UH-60A Tactical Helicopter

Mechanic training

Mar-Oct 1983: Ft Lewis, WA. UH-60A Blackhawk mechanic and

Crewchief; two training exercises at Yakama Training Center,

Yakama, WA. One training exercise at Moses Lake, WA

Oct 1983-Sep 1984: Ft Rucker, AL. Warrant Officer Flight

Training student

Sep 1984-Dec 1984: Ft Rucker, AL. AH-1F Cobra pilot qualification

Jan 1985-Dec 1985: Camp LaGuardia, Republic of Korea, AH-1F

Cobra pilot and Air Cavalry pilot with 4/7 Air Cavalry Squadron

Jan 1986-Jul 1987: Ft Bragg, NC. AH-1F Cobra pilot and Attack

Helicopter Pilot, 1/82nd Attack Battalion; one training exercise at Ft AP Hill, VA where I won the TOP Cobra Crew award along with my commander; one exercise to the Army's National Training Center (Desert training) Barstow, CA; two trips to Corpus Christi Naval Air Station to turn in the Attack Battalion's AH-1Fs in preparation for getting the new AH-64s (the trips took 2 days each to fly from Ft Bragg to Corpus Christi and we never got above 500' above the ground, normal Helicopter altitudes); three weeks at Ft Benning for Basic Parachutist training.

July 1987- Sep 1988: Ft Bragg, NC. AH-1S Cobra pilot and Air Cavalry pilot with 1/17 Air Cavalry Squadron; one training week at Ft Campbell, KY for AH-1 Simulator Instructor course; one training exercise at Camp Lejuene, NC. to support 82nd troops working with Marines; one training exercise at Ft Drum, NY to support the 10th Mountain Division troops because they didn't have their own aviation assets; one training exercise at Tweny-nine Palms Marine Corps training station supporting 82nd and Egyptian troops (I was called off of leave to support this exercise because one of my sister troops didn't have any pilots who had flown in Mountain Desert environment).

I mentioned before I would discuss how God intervened and worked in my life to get me from the farm on track to going to the Air Force. Every position I had and every place I went was a building block for the next thing I did.

One example was that being an enlisted mechanic made me a better officer and pilot. My time as a helicopter pilot made me a better fixed wing/fighter pilot.

I mentioned I had applied for WOFT training out of high school but was made an alternate. I look back and truly know that God knew I was too immature to go straight to WOFT. I believe I would have made it through flight training but I would not have been a good officer. I needed to be enlisted and become a mechanic because it helped mature me and made me a better officer and pilot. Had I gone to Ft Campbell versus Ft Lewis, I would have been put a year behind applying for WOFT. At Ft Lewis I was allowed to apply on day one. Ft Campbell had a policy you had to be on station a year before you could apply for WOFT. God allowed me to leave Ft Lewis at the right time because 1) the group of friends I got to make in my 84-11 Purple Flight class at WOFT were the best of the best people to be around and 2) a month after I left Ft Lewis the UH-60 I was responsible for and the crew chief on crashed during a NVG training mission and killed all 4 crew members onboard. Going to Korea versus anywhere else allowed me to advance faster as a Cobra pilot.

Getting the opportunity to be assigned to D Troop 4/7th Cavalry in Korea allowed me to learn from seasoned combat veterans and be near an education center to take CLEP tests and earn 36 college credits. Not being allowed to extend for 6 months in Korea put me on track to complete most of my college night school and put me on a collision course to meet my future wife at the right time and the place, all in God's timing (I believe we almost crossed paths 2 years before at Pensacola Naval Air Station, but it was not at the right time). Getting assigned to B Company 1/82nd Attack Battalion allowed me to serve under a commander that gave me the opportunity to take as many night classes as I could as long as it didn't interfere with my flying missions. Going to parachutist training and parachuting in the the 82nd paid big dividends six years later when I came back to Ft Bragg as an Air Force pilot assigned to be an Air Liaison Officer/Forward Air Controller (ALO/FAC). God's timing was perfect and His hands were guiding me even though many times I was trying to go a different direction.

How did you decide to switch from the Army to the Air Force?

⬥

I believe this question could actually be split in two questions: how did I decide and why did I decide?

The "how" was pretty easy. After all my applications to the AF, Navy, MD State Patrol, NC and SC Army Guard units, the Air Force is the organization that called first and offered me a position. The Navy called a week later and the other 3 called within 2 weeks. Plus Pam had said she would be OK with the Navy if I "didn't" get into the Air Force. I relished the thought of being catapulted from an Aircraft Carrier but I knew life in the Air Force would be much better for having a family and children.

The "why" will take a bit to explain. I originally only planned to do my 4 years of flying in the Army and either going back to Nebraska to fly Crop dusters or go back and teach at Ft Rucker, AL as a contractor and try to fly in the Alabama Air Guard that was getting F-16s (a friend of my brother David was in that unit). But as I got married and saw more of all the different services and saw Fighter jets flying in person I thought that would be pretty cool. Plus my brother David would constantly tell me that "anyone can fly helos, only real pilots flew jets." So I figured that since I was getting my degree anyway I would at least apply to the AF, Navy and Marine Corps and see what happens. Ended up the AF and Navy had the same policy that I could submit my application when I could show them I had less than a year left in the Army. My real dream aircraft was the Marine AV-8 Harrier, but the Marine Corps policy was that I had to be completely out of the Army to submit my application. I asked the recruiter how long after I submit my application would I hear back whether I got in? He said 4-6 months. I said Ok, then if I get selected, how long would it be before I would start training and get a pay check? He said 4-6 months more. I said, so it could be a year from me getting out of the Army to getting to start in the Marines, I don't need to fly the Harrier that bad. All my other job prospects would basically allow me to go from being in the Army one day and the next start the new job the next.

Looking back I can't imagine any of the other choices being better than the path God laid out for me. Having the Air Force call before all the others made the decision that much easier.

What did you do in the Air Force?

This section will take a little longer than the Army section because I spent twice as much time in the Air Force Active Duty and I will include my time in the North Carolina Air National Guard (NC ANG). I did 6 years in the Army, 14.5 years in the Active Duty Air Force, and 9.5 years in the Air National Guard.

This is the path I took: Officer Training School (OTS) Medina Annex, San Antonio, TX; Air Force Undergraduate Pilot Training (UPT) at Vance AFB, OK; F-16C Training at McDill AFB, FL; F-16C pilot at Homestead AFB, FL; Air Liaison Officer/Forward Air Controller (ALO/FAC) at Pope AFB/Ft Bragg, NC; F-15E Training at Seymour-Johnson AFB, NC; F-15E pilot at Royal Air Force Base (RAF) Lakenheath, UK; T-37 Pilot Instructor Training (PIT) at Randolph AFB, TX; T-37 Instructor at Columbus AFB, MS; T-6A PIT back at Randolph AFB, TX: T-6A Instructor at Moody AFB, GA; ALO/FAC at Stanley County Airport, NC (Air National Guard).

After 6 years in the Army I drove to San Antonio TX, to start Air Force Officer Training School (OTS). After having completed Army Basic training and WOFT I figured OTS would be cinch, but I would soon find out OTS would be difficult in its own way. In the Army if you could max out your physical fitness test they didn't care how well you did on the academic test (which weren't so difficult) and all you needed to pass an academic test was a 70% (normally every test had 50 questions. We joked about tests being Seven O and Go, or 85 + or - 15). But the Air Force was 180 degrees out. They were happy with a minimum passing score on the Physical Fitness test of 70% (on a very easy Fitness test at that). But on academic tests you had to have passing scores of 85% on tests that usually only had 20-25 questions which meant you could only miss 2 questions and academics were very heavy on writing and producing reports and papers on subjects. Most tests weren't just True/False, most were "What is the most correct answer?". In the Army most of the questions were like "What color are Army helicopters?" or "If you are heading South, what cardinal direction is to your left?" But after 3 months I graduated with a 95% academic average and 125% on the Physical Fitness test. I was commissioned as an AF 2nd Lieutenant and was off to Vance AFB outside Enid, OK for Air Force Fixed-wing pilot training (UPT).

We started UPT with 24 students and graduated 15 (13 were original students). We had basic flying academics along with Ejection seat training, Parachute training, Altitude Chamber training, and some other training to prepare us to start flying the T-37 (also known as the Tweet or the 6,000 pound Dog Whistle because of the high pitched noise it made when the engines were running). The the T-37 was a small twin engine, side-by-side seating jet that was designed and built in the 1960s. For the next 5 months we learned how to fly Acrobatics, Instruments, Formation, and Visual navigation. Having already earned my Fixed wing pilot license and 1,200 flight hours in helicopters the training was fun and relatively easy.

Following T-37 training we, moved on to supersonic twin engine jet training in the T-38 Talon. In the T-37, students were taught the basics of flying. T-38 students were taught how to do those things at much higher speeds. For the next 6 months we showed our instructors we could handle the speeds and G-forces that went along with high speeds while flying Instruments and close formation flying. With 6 weeks to graduation, we submitted what aircraft we wanted to fly after graduation and I put F-16 or the A-10. I ended up graduating No 1 in my class and was also assigned an F-16 with a training class at MacDill, AFB in Tampa, FL.

Following UPT graduation, I headed to Holloman AFB, NM where our class of 20 students from all 5 different UPT training bases were taught Basic Fighter pilot skills in a modified T-38 called the AT-38. This allowed us to learn Air-to-Air and Air-to-Ground skills in a cheap, familiar aircraft before we moved onto the more expensive front line fighter aircraft.

After 3 months of training I met Pam, Daniel and (Andrew - Pam was 6 months pregnant) at MacDill AFB to start F-16 training. For the next 6 months our class of 16 students expanded on the basic fighter skills we learned in the AT-38 in a multi-million dollar front line fight. The F-16 was designed as a cheap day time fighter-bomber that could engage the evil Soviet Fighters and Bombers in Air Combat and deliver near precision bombs on enemy targets all while evading a phalanx of Surface-to-Air missiles designed to blow American fighter jets out of the sky. The F-16 actually was a relatively easy aircraft to fly (the designers want an easy aircraft to fly so the pilot could concentrate on performing the missions). It was easy to maneuver onto the ground targets but very fast and we had to not only learn to fly in formations of 2 or 4, but in formations of 12 to 24 aircraft. With about about 2 months left in training we submitted requests for where to be stationed following graduation. I had hoped to go to Spangdelhem Air Base Germany but since our class only had 2 slots for that base, 2 senior officers in the class got that. I then hoped to go to Moody AFB, GA but another senior officer got that slot. So with 2 slots to Homestead AFB and 8 slots to Korea and Japan, Homestead for me was the best option available. Homestead AFB is where Pam, Daniel, newborn Andrew, and I would be heading following 3 weeks of AF Survival/POW training at Fairchild AFB outside Spokane, WA.

Let me add that Iraq invaded Kuwait in September of 1990 while I was at in F-16 training and the night before we graduated POW training Operation Desert Shield turned into Operation Desert Storm that began with hundreds of US fighters and bombers crossing Iraq and Kuwait borders the first night of wave after wave of bombing missions to kick Saddam Hussein's military out of Kuwait.

On my way to Homestead AFB that following week I was informed my unit the 308th Fighter Squadron would be deploying soon to the Middle East in support of Desert Storm. I was actually very excited about getting the opportunity to get to do what I had trained for but by the time I arrived the 308th FS was taken off the list of deployment because they had some of the oldest F-16s (Block 15s) in the Air Force. Within a week of my arrival it was announced the 308th FS would be getting the newest F-16s (Block 40s) with the ability to do fly night missions using terrain following and drop laser guided bombs with a targeting pod (in 1990 less than 10% of AF fighters had this, in 2023: 100% of fighters have them). So over the next few months all the pilots went to Luke AFB and got qualified in the new F-16 Block 40s and we start taking delivery of brand new jets. During the next year we trained up to deploy to Bergan Air Base, Flesland, Norway for a month of training in Europe as part of what was called Checkered Flag. Checkered Flags were designed to familiarize fighter squadrons in the US with European bases they would be deployed in the event of WW3 with the Soviet Union. For a month we ate lots of reindeer meat and flew missions throughout Europe, training and getting familiar with the area.

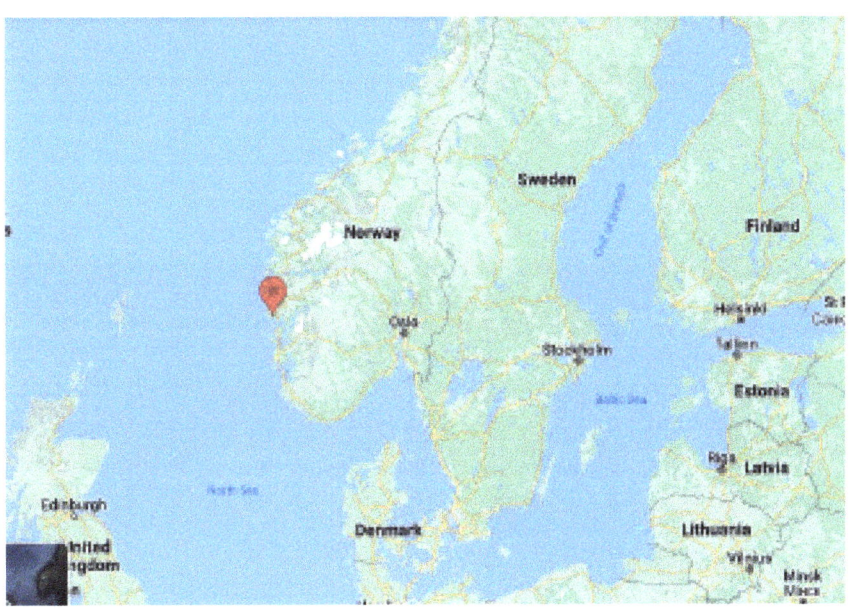

In Norway on a Checkered Flag exercise from Homestead AFB, FL

Getting into position to aerial refuel.

With Andrew and Daniel when I returned from Norway.

During the rest of my tour at Homestead I went on two 3 week exercises to Nellis AFB, Las Vegas, NV. and a week long exercise to Seymour-Johnson AFB, NC.

Papa and Gma and friends at Seymour-Johnson AFB when I did an exercise with the F-15E squadrons Between exercises, I flew about 3 days a week doing both Air-to-Air training and Air-to-Ground training. As Andrew's 2nd birthday was approaching we were looking towards the next year and a possible 4 month deployment to Operation Southern Watch where we were to deploy to Saudi Arabia and fly missions over the southern half of Iraq. Weeeelllll, on a Friday in late August 1992 our squadron had our annual Hurricane Season briefing where we were informed a small Cat I hurricane named ANDREW that was in NO WAY going to hit South Florida and was turning north toward Bermuda. Within 2 hours ANDREW made a hard turn directly towards Homestead and became a Cat II hurricane and we were told to prepare to evacuate. Saturday night we loaded the Ford Explorer with gas, photos, kids and dog (Hart) and Pam prepared to drive to Rocky Mount. Sunday morning I flew an F-16 Shaw AFB, SC and my sister Cynthia picked me up so I could watch the ANDREW destroy Homestead

AFB on CNN.

At Homestead AFB with the aircraft's crewchief.

After a couple of days CNN showed the destruction of Homestead AFB and we knew we were not returning to fly there again. Pam and I returned with her dad and my brother Mark's help and loaded what was left of our household goods. At this same time the Air Force was in dire need of Air Liaison Officers/Forward Air Controllers (ALO/FACs), especially those willing to parachute with the 82nd Air Borne Division at Ft Bragg, NC and the 3

Army Ranger Battalions. Since I was already military parachute qualified and Ft Bragg was located within 2 hours of Rocky Mount, I made the Fighter Branch flesh peddler (Personnel manager) extremely happy that I was volunteering to fill one of those hard to fill positions. So off to Hurlburt AFB, FL for 3 weeks of ALO/FAC training and then off to AF Detachment 1, 507 Air Control Wing, Ft Bragg, NC. Normally most new ALO/FACs spend 2-3 months of training at Ft Bragg before they are sent alone to work with their assigned Army unit. After 2 days in the unit I was sent alone to work with the same 82nd Attack Helicopter Battalion I had been part of just 5 years earlier (several enlisted men were still in that unit) because I had enough experience with the Army (Duugghh). Over the next 2.5 years we trained and parachuted and trained some more. The actual ALO position required Majors (O-4) because of the requirement to work with Army Colonels (O-6) and Generals (O-7 to O-10), but few AF Majors want to parachute so most of the ALOs in our unit were young Captains (O-3). When I arrived the unit was still recovering from their participation in Desert Storm so there wasn't a lot of training. The unit was down to only doing 160 Close Air Support (CAS) missions a year or about 14 missions a month and on average two parachute jump training missions a month. Within one year, myself and the other young captains had ramped up CAS missions to over 1,500 a year and two parachute missions per a week. I also supported Joint Special Operations Command (JSOC) training and operations when they needed extra ALO/FACs.

Getting ready to load a C-130 for a combat jump into Port-a-Prince, Haiti

After a parachute jump at Ft Pickett, VA. We worked out great training opportunities with Mr Gary Watts, the Ft Pickett manager, since it was a National Guard base and wasn't used much outside of the summer. Mr Watts said we could also integrate with the Army Guard units in the summer and teach them how to incorporate CAS missions with their Artillery training and Infantry training. So we worked out missions where we would parachute in and control CAS missions for 2-3 days. We would also take Army Special Forces and Marine units with us and we would train them on Emergency CAS and then run parachute jumps when not doing CAS training.

Getting ready to control some Close Air Support (CAS) aircraft at Ft Pickett, VA. Daniel and Andrew went with me once for 4 days and they got to drive a HUMMV like this.

As I was finishing up my tour as an ALO/FAC, I went to Maxwell AFB, AL for 6 weeks of Officer Training, but I was recalled back to Ft Bragg to head up the Air Power portion of Operation Restore Democracy (Airborne Assault into Port-a-Prince, Haiti). Pam was surprised when I came home and I wasn't able to tell her why and I couldn't tell her why I was getting all my combat gear ready. I spent the next 5 days working with 18th Airborne Corps Commander (General Shelton and his staff), 82nd Airborne Division Commander and his staff, and 8 different Air Force unit commanders (C-130, AC-130, A-10, F-15, AF Weather, 12th Air Force Staff) on how we were going to integrate jet fighters and Army helicopters in the Ground battle plan. The airlift side had been planning for 9 months (only a few knew that) how they were going get Sixty-plus C-130s, C-141s and C-5s loaded with paratroopers and equipment and amassed over Haiti for the largest Airborne Parachute operation since WWII D-Day. We also coordinated with Delta Force leaders on how we would support their operations of capturing the Haiti President and Vice President (both evil and corrupt men).

When my tour was over I headed to Seymour-Johnson AFB, NC about an hour away to learn how to fly the F-15E Strike Eagle. It was twice the size of the F-16 and carried a pilot and a Weapon Systems Officer (WSO) and twice the bomb load of the F-16. It was designed to be an all-weather night bomber to replace the F-111. Following training completion, I headed to RAF Lakenheath, UK to find a house for Pam and the boys to join me there.

I signed into the 492nd Fighter Squadron, The Bowlers, and soon became a squadron scheduler and flight lead.

Bowler hat like we wore to show we were in the 492nd FS.

At Lakenheath AFB with an F-15E

While at RAF Lakenheath we trained to do Air-to-Air combat and Day/Night Precision bombing with laser designating targeting pods. We deployed twice to Incerlik, Turkey to enforce the No-Fly Zone over Northern Iraq (Northern Watch). Near the end of our tour at RAF Lakenheath we supported the missions over Yugoslavia.

Incerlik Air Base, Turkey.

We returned to the States and I became a T-37 Tweet primary pilot Training Instructor. I completed the 3 month school at Randolph AFB, San Antonio, TX in 5 weeks and we arrived at Columbus AFB, MS to start our tour there. I did a couple of months as a line instructor in Delta Flight then took over Mustang Flight as it's Commander. We trained new students how to fly acrobatics, instruments, and formation flight. I finished up one class of students from start to finish and started up a new class when I was selected to become the Chief of all T-37 training at Columbus. This job entailed me overseeing the standardization and training of all two hundred T-37 Instructor Pilots and teaching and running the Wings SPIN Training program.

Pam, Me, Daniel, Andrew, and Turner in from of the Mighty Tweet

Picking up a brand new T-6A from Beech Aircraft in Wichita, KS and flying it to Moody AFB, GA. I probably picked up and flew more new aircraft than anyone else because I was one of only a few qualified to do so. Plus Pam and the Boys were still at Columbus AFB, MS so I was free to travel more than anyone else.

With about 2 years to go of my 20 year military career I was selected to be part of the initial cadre for the Air Force's newest trainer, the T-6A. The T-6 was a replacement for the T-37 so we did all the same kind of training in it that we did in the Tweet.

After I retired from 20.5 years of active duty, I was one of two officers to be selected for a new program that allowed active duty retirees to join the AF Reserves and Air National Guard (ANG). Since I had been an ALO/FAC and the North Carolina ANG needed pilots with my experience I was quickly brought in. I was immediately made the Operations Officer and started to train our part-time (traditional Guardsmen) how to operate with the Army units we supported and how to effectively control CAS missions. With my background of F-16s and F-15Es, I quickly started working with Fighters from Shaw AFB and Seymour-Johnson AFB to do CAS missions. I also contacted Mr. Gary Watts at Ft Pickett, VA and set up training opportunities for Close Quarters Maneuvering (House Clearing) and parachute operations and CAS training. Also, every February the Canadian Army National Guard from Nova Scotia came to Ft Pickett, VA and we would work with them during their two weeks of Annual Training. I had only planned to do a couple of years in the ANG, but since it was pretty much one weekend a month I ended up doing 9.5 years (but only added up to 2.3 years of actual time). Pam told me once that I couldn't quit the military cold turkey and she was right. God worked it out for me to ease my way out and when I was done, I was ready to be done. I ended up getting activated and deploying to Iraq with the NC Army National Guard and staying and working with an active duty unit, 3rd Brigade, 1st Infantry Division. I helped plan and execute a two week Air Support mission called "Seeds of Liberty Routes."

What was it like being in a war?

You probably have heard me or someone else say; "it's hours of sheer boredom interrupted by moments of sheer terror."

Before I start writing I want to say that that compared to what my dad and others like him in WW2, Korea, and Vietnam experienced my experience was nothing near that. But the one thing I have in common with them is that there are always weird, sometimes unexplainable, and sometimes funny things that happen that just make you say "Hmmmmm."

Part of what military training does is prepare and desensitize troops to what real war is. Looking back over 30 years of serving I can honestly say I am thankful I never had to drop a bomb or shoot the enemy. I had many opportunities and came very close but I ended up not needing to do it. Most join the combatant units in the military with the knowledge that they may have to do what it takes to stop an enemy. Most are chomping at the bit after many months of training to do their jobs and most are relieved then they are done that they didn't end having to, but were ready.

In the 1960s and 70s the Soviets were an easy enemy to hate during the Cold War and millions of men and women joined, served and were ready to die to defend our freedoms. Most knew that if a real war broke out in Europe, it would get ugly very quick and most of those stationed in Germany would be killed in the first month of a conflict as units in the States mobilized to get across the Atlantic to fight the evil Communists. US Air Force Nuclear Bomber crews knew that if they launched over the North Pole to strike into Russia that they were making a oneway trip. Actual combat in Korea and Vietnam placed much more mental stress on troops because they were in constant fear of enemy activity where as during the Cold War it was more of a concept as to what it would be like if war broke out.

As for what it was like for me and those who served around me, we were very focused and prepared every minute the first month. The next couple months we were probably a little too complacent and didn't think anything would happen, and then the last couple weeks were were really stressed thinking; "Man, it would be awful to have something happen the last few days were there." In February 2005, the last week I was in Iraq, six Army soldiers in the brigade I supported drowned in a vehicle accident. Very sad and I had two F-15Es overhead the scene prepared to keep the enemy away if they tried something. We all just couldn't believe what had happened and felt helpless.

The picture of me with a parachute was from September 1994 when we were going to make a combat parachute jump onto the Porte-A-Prince, Haiti airport runway. I was the lead Air Force officer among the twelve C-130s carrying 700 Airborne troops followed by 1,200 more troops who were to parachute into an open field one mile from the airfield. Our twelve C-130s were following twelve C-130s with eleven M551 Sheridan Tanks and one Air Force HUMMV radio system (mine). We had about 100 Air Force Forward Air Controllers and enlisted

Airmen on the operation for which the previous week I spent with the Army leadership planning the mission to capture Haiti's President and Vice President and secure the city of Porte-A-Prince and surrounding area. We ended up not jumping but the all the training we had done prior prepared us well. I was wasn't nervous and I had a pretty good idea of how everything would happen. At the same time we were all hopped up and excited and rearing to jump. When the jump was called off (we were just north of Miami, FL), as soon as everyone got the word on my aircraft they almost instantly fell asleep from being being high on adrenaline for the previous 10 hours.

The picture below of me next to an F-15E was during a Operation Northern Watch mission. I was stationed at RAF Lakaenheath and we deployed for three months to Incerlik Air Base, Turkey. We were there to protect the Iraqi Kurds from Saddam Hussein. We would fly daily missions over Northern Iraq and were prepared to attack Iraqi forces if they threatened the Kurds. We didn't drop any bombs, but was prepared to do so.

Combat is a lot like sports (except a lot higher chance of getting shot). As you get closer to starting the game or match, your brain starts going through every possible situation and the adrenaline starts to get you excited and ready to go.

Most combatants will tell you that combat isn't just hardship, danger and fear, but there are sometimes many things that happen that on one hand can be really dangerous, but at the same time very funny and can be told over and over again at reunions and cause everyone to laugh again and again even while recognizing the disaster the incident could have caused had it been slightly different. A good example of this was on one of the twelve personnel C-130s. Soon after the word was spread that that Operation "Just Kidding" (our joking name for it) was cancelled and we were turning around and heading back to Ft Bragg/Pope AFB, two young Army privates (we had several privates who had graduated high school in early June, went immediately to Infantry Basic Training and right into Army Parachute School and now only a few weeks after arrival to Ft Bragg were making a Combat Jump), raised their hands. When their Platoon Sergeant asked them what they wanted they said "Sergeant, what do we do with our Hand Grenades?" To which the Sergeant replied "Keep them in your pouches on your utility belt!" One of the Privates said "But Sergeant, we already pulled the pins on the grenades!" The Air Force Load Master heard this and grabbed some safety wire and leaped across several seated paratroopers and fussed out the Privates out as he safety wired the grenades. You might we wondering why these young knuckleheads pulled the pins on their grenades? Well, having pulled many pins on Smoke grenades and a few hand grenades, these pins are very hard to extract. Unlike the movies where some guys use their teeth to pull the pins, in real life they would have broken their teeth.

Down below is a picture of my talking to a soldier in a beard. He was an Australian SAS (Special Air Service/their version of Delta Force) and it was the summer of 2002. I had moved Pam and the kids to Rocky Mount so Daniel could start his high school freshman year and I then deployed to Kuwait to help with the build up and training for an invasion into Iraq (the original plan was to invade in September as the 120 degree temps decreased, but Congress stepped in and caused a 6 month wait). While I was there at Camp Doha (Kuwait City), I was tasked to provide Air Strike training in the Kuwaiti desert to US and Foreign troops before they went into Afghanistan. Because of the rugged terrain in Afghanistan, we had to train the troops to use newer radio and laser rangefinder equipment. Then we escorted them to Afghanistan and provided them with some in-country orientation.

In 2004 just after Thanksgiving I deployed to Northern Baghdad, Iraq to support the North Carolina Army National Guard as an Air Liaison Officer/FAC. The NC Guard ended up leaving a month early so I ended up moving to Baquba (Ba-qu-ba) which was just north of Baghdad and was the home to many foreign fighters. As January 2005 rolled around we started to prepare for their first ever election. Leading up to the election, at our weekly staff meetings we were alway informed that at least one of the 30 Iraqis running in our 200 square mile sector from local mayor to national congress was either killed or wounded and that someone else was willing to run in their place. (Now how many of our elected officials do you think would continue with their campaigns if there was a chance to get wounded or killed?) I set up a schedule and flight route for fighter support for the week leading up to the election to let the good Iraqis know we were there to help and the Bad Guys know we were ready for them. The day before the election our base was hit by a couple of mortar rounds and our counter battery radar pin pointed the spot it came from and I had two F-15Es at the location in 5 minutes. But once they got to the open field all they saw were six guys in a truck about 300 yards from the firing point. We were ready to drop on them but the Army commander was afraid with the election the next day that the US Press would spin it out of control. So we tracked them to a farm and when the truck stopped all the men jumped out and ran six different ways. I got up at 4:30AM the next morning and prepared to what we thought would be "all Hell breaking loose." During the previous week the Army had fortified all the voting locations and had put troops at each one. (I believe we had 150 sites to cover). Voting sites were to open at 7:30AM and at 7AM my radio started to crackle with an Army Captain screaming on my radio that a large mob was heading toward them and that we need to stop them with Air Power. I had a set of F-15Es overhead in one minute and they described a mob of about 70 people filling the streets and heading in the Army captain's direction. I asked the fighters if they saw any weapons, they said no, then one of the fighter pilots said "they seem to be stopping at moving in a single file toward a building at Such-n-Such location, what is there?" I looked at my map and said "It's a voting location", The pilot said "It looks like whole families with kids going to vote." We had no idea that because they wanted to vote so bad that they would overcome their fear of danger and felt that going as a large group their chances of survival was much higher. 95% of Iraqs eligible to vote went out that single day to vote (2 months prior in the US less than 40% turned out). 95% knowing they could be shot or blown up versus 40% and our only fear was getting rained on (very sad). I can't believe how close we came to dropping 500lbs bombs on men and women and children who were just out to vote. God saved us that day and I am thankful.

On the ramp at Pope AFB about to load a C-130 heading to make a combat parachute jump in Porte-a-Prince, Haiti September of 1994.

Loaded and preflighting on an Operation Northern Watch mission. We flew into Northern Iraq from Incerlik Air Base, Turkey.

Summer of 2002 in Kuwait teaching Australian SAS (special ops) how to call in air strikes. When I finished their training I went to Afghanistan with them for a few days to provide them with an in-country orientation.

Bagram, Afghanistan summer of 2002.

On my C-17 flight back to Kuwait from Afghanistan. The C-17 pilot to my right was one of my students when I taught at Columbus AFB, MS.

What is it like being an airline pilot for Southwest?

I jokingly tell people that my kids associate flying with being gone all the time. Oh wait, that is what flying has meant for most of my 41 year flying career and even more so in the airline industry.

Before I get into what it's like being an airline pilot for Southwest, I need to mention two things. 1. For most of my life and military career I had no intention or desire to be an airline pilot because I thought it would be boring and I would be gone a lot, plus I truly didn't understand what being an airline pilot would be like (probably because I didn't know anyone who was an airline pilot.) 2. In early 1999, less than 2 years before I submitted an application to Southwest, I had zero actual knowledge of the company, its operation, nor where they flew. I met a senior Southwest pilot and after spending two hours discussing Southwest, I literally looked him in the eye and said, "Wow sounds like a great company but I don't want to live in Texas." (I had no idea they flew out of the state of Texas) If you ever saw the movie "Officer and Gentleman" (it was an ok movie), there is a scene where the tough Officer Training Drill Sergeant is trying to the get the lead actor (who is a Officer Trainee) to quit Officer training by hosing him down with a water hose while the Trainee is doing pushups and sit-ups to exhaustion. The Drill Sergeant yells at him, "Why are you here, you don't want to be here, just quit." The Trainee yells several times, "I want to fly jets, Drill Sergeant", but when close to total exhaustion the Trainee finally breaks down almost crying and yells, "I've got no where else to go!" The Sergeant now having finally broke the stubborn Trainee's arrogant attitude down, says back, "Ok, you can go back to your class now," and the Trainee gets to graduate. What does this have to do with why I became an airline pilot?

Well....... after about 10 years in the military I had thought after completing my 20 years I would go into teaching at a local school and be home every night. But as I got to my 18 year point I started to realize I didn't have many civilian skills. There's not a lot of need for someone who could drop bombs or parachute out of an airplane or shoot an M-16. I also met some pilots who were going to the airlines or who were current airline pilots. I looked back on my days as an ALO/FAC (non-flying) and realized that, like being an ALO/FAC, a job as a teacher could be rewarding but a lot of work. I enjoyed my time as an ALO/FAC but because we wore Army fatigues and not a flight suits we were treated like second-class citizens in the Air Force. I realized that because wearing flight suit quickly identified me as a pilot and for some reason everyone on base treated me much better even though being an ALO/FAC had a lot more responsibility and was much more demanding. (Yes, I am very shallow and enjoyed being OOHed and AHHed just for wearing a flight suit).

As I contemplated what to do, I started to realize "I HAD NOWHERE ELSE TO GO." So on 1 September 2001, I submitted my applications to Southwest Airlines and JetBlue Airlines and was planning to apply to Delta, American, and UPS. Then the attacks on 9/11 (September

11, 2001) happened and within days thousands of airline pilots were out of jobs at all the companies except JetBlue and Southwest. I immediately thought that since I am leaving the Air Force in a year and I need a back up plan, maybe teaching will be it. North Carolina had a Lateral Entry teaching program. Then by God's grace in mid-October 2001, JetBlue's CEO called (they were still very small with only 17 airplanes) and he did a mini-phone pre-interview. At the end of the interview, I asked him if he understood I still had about 11 months left in the Air Force. He said "I'm sorry. We thought you were out already. Can we call you in April 2002 to start the interview process? (First off, I was shocked any airline called just after 9/11, but I had also heard JetBlue liked to start you in training within 4 months of the interview). Then the first week of December 2001, Southwest's People Department called and said they are starting to interview the first week of January 2002 for 3 weeks of interviews. They asked me when I would like to interview. (I had been told to take the first possible Monday morning interview because if you wait until the Friday, the interviewers are tired and they have a lot of pilots to compare you to, where as Mondays they are fresh and happy and have no comparison). I picked 7 January 2002. I had my Boeing 737 type rating. I paid $8,400 for the training and hotel in the summer of 2000 because I had never flown a big jet and wanted to see if I would be good at it. I thought that there was a chance I was going to be sent to Korea on a non-flying staff job when I finished my tour at Columbus AFB versus Moody AFB and didn't want to try to do the training after not flying for a over a year. I had paid $500 for Interview Preparation and $1,200 in new dress suits and showed up to SWA headquarters at Love Field ready to go. I guess my interview went well and was told I was hired a month later on 8 February 2002 and would be given a training date when I finished up my time in the Air

Force. Since the economy didn't get better for almost two years, I finally started SWA training 15 March 2004. I did 8 more months in the Air Force and then 7 months teaching middle school and worked for my brother Mark's company in Saudi Arabia teaching Saudi pilots in the Simulator. I spent almost 5 months working as a security guard for Walmart in Greenville and a precious metals smelting plant in Greenville during that 2 years.

Sooooo, what is it like being a Southwest Airlines (SWA) pilot? The first thing I learned was that SWA puts a lot of trust in and expected a lot of work out of its pilots. When I say "trust", I mean they trust you to do your job and get to work on time and get the passengers to where they want to go on time (or as close as possible). At the end of a 3 or 4 day trip you just walk off the airplane and no one calls you to see how it went and you don't have to call anyone to get permission to leave. A big change from the military where you always had to report in after landing and ask permission to leave if you got done early. I have heard that at other airlines they treat the pilots like the military does. As for work load expected from the pilots, in the military we normally worked 250-280 days (8-10 hours each day) during the year and the. average amount of flying I did was about 1-2 hours each day of the 160-200 days I actually flew (average year of flying was between 200-250 hours). The rest of the day was spent briefing before and debriefing after the flight training. The days we didn't fly (other than the weekends) we did busy work as a junior pilot and actually completed paperwork or staff meetings as a senior pilot. At SWA, I average 200-230 days a year at work and fly 700-900 hours a year (I'm only paid for the time I'm flying or in the simulator). My busiest year I flew 995 hours. FAA regulations only allow you to fly a maximum of 1000 hours per year. At the other airlines they average 230-250 days of work but only fly 400-600 hours a year. They do a lot of sitting around and waiting between flights because of their Hub and Spoke system and the fact that they have 15 pilots per airplane and we only have 12 pilots per airplane but fly more and haul more passengers than they do. Their pilots brag about how little they fly (you never hear them discuss how many days a month they work). SWA pilot schedules are a lot more productive and we can make as much money as they do in few days. This means that if you want to increase your pay you have a couple extra days a month to fly extra. But overall the physical part of flying for SWA is not really much different than flying other aircraft. Ok maybe a little boring because I don't drop bombs or shoot a Gatling gun at anything, but we do fly into way worse weather than we did in the Air Force because people want to get to their destinations.

We do get paid pretty well, but we are also away from home 220ish days a year. For example, a three day trip I might get paid for 18 hours of work but I was away from home for 72 hours. Most people can't conceive of that and that's why I tell people SWA pay me 25% of my pay for working and 75% of my pay to be away from my family. It's a job you really have to love to do and have a spouse and children that won't hold it against you (SWA pilot divorce rate is lower than other companies, but has increased over the past several years.

What is it like to be an airline pilot here at SWA? I will admit that most of the kids we fly think we are pretty cool and most of the passengers believe we are really good at our jobs (some adults think we are pretty cool also). So from an ego perspective our egos are pumped up pretty well by the passengers. The company has a lot of departments (like Planning, Training, Dispatch and Scheduling) that do a lot of the work I would have had to do in the Air Force. Hotel vans are waiting for us when we arrive for the night and hotels treat us really well because our company spends a lot of money there.

As a SWA Check Airman, I am held to even higher standards (and pedestal) by the other pilots and SWA itself. I get paid a little extra but have more paperwork to do and have a lot more responsibility. Out of 10,000 SWA pilots, we only have 400 pilots designated by the FAA as Check Airman. We are responsible for training new SWA First Officers and Captains and annual evaluations. Now most new First Officers come to us with 2,000-6,000 hours of flight experience. We train them in our way of doing business and in the Boeing 737. There are hundreds of SWA pilots who would probably be better Check Airmen than me and many of the other Check Airmen, but they prefer to have more flexibility in their monthly schedule or don't like dealing with running simulators for evaluations. We are kind of like the State Highway Patrol. Everyone tries to avoid them but at the same time glad they are doing their jobs as long as they don't bother you and give you a ticket. Overall, being a Check Airman is a lot like what I did as an Instructor Evaluator at Columbus AFB and Moody AFB but I have a lot more flexibility and authority to get the job done. For example, several times when I needed a flight held for me or I needed to switch airplanes or flights because my route wasn't going to work I made a call to Scheduling or Dispatch and told them what I needed and they did it without question (regular Captains rarely can do that).

PROs: Cool job, great view from the window, great pay, pretty good travel benefits (poor compared to Delta and United but we don't travel much), great coworkers, hands-off bosses.

CONs: Many days away from home, over regulated by the FAA, longs days when the weather is bad, annual evaluations, cranky passengers when the WiFi is inoperative or we are late, way too many nights in different hotels, high cost of food on the road (we do get $50 per day per diem that normally covers most of my meals).

Basically: "I've got nowhere else to go". Haha

Only Check Airmen got to fly the MAX-8 first

MAX-8 Cockpit

Flight Testing a MAX-8 without passengers

Me and another Check Airman

What hobbies did you have as a kid?

My hobbies as a child from ages 5-10 were playing "Nebraska Football" (pretending to be a NE football player), playing "War" (lots of WW2 movies and sister Kathy and brother Tom were in the Army in Vietnam 1969 and 1970), and making "Movies" (we pretended to make movies in our hay bar). Also I enjoyed making kites to fly, out of long sticks and paper from 55lbs grain supplement sacks (kind of like dog food bags we emptied out when we mixed it with our grain for the milk cows).

From ages 10 and older my hobbies were making wooden swords out of long sticks we pulled out of fencing that was used to stop snow from driving on the roads in the area. I always assumed a couple sticks here and there missing wouldn't cause the snow to drift too much. I also enjoyed making bows and arrows to play with. As we got to our teens, my brother Mark and I started to go hunting pheasant and quail in the winter time and if we saw rabbits we would shoot them. We rarely had extra shotgun ammunition to practice with but every now and then we would buy some clay pidgins and hand throw them.

In high school we fixed up my Grandpa DeWald's old 1947 Willys Jeep to drive around and a couple of old cars and trucks. I got interested in photography and learned how to develop my own film and black and white prints. B&W is very easy with very few chemicals required. Color requires a ton of chemicals and effort.

Pam

Interesting!

What are your top favorite books?

Wonderful question:

1. The Bible – God's Holy word

2. As an 8th grader my favorite was Sir MacHinery It looks funnybecause it is Machinery. It is not as sophisticated as I remember but it was totally original and in an odd way wonderful in the sense of good triumphing over evil. The plot is simple and stereotypical, but classic. The idea of a robot, a wizard, and the modern man teaming together to fight demons just gives you a marvelous feeling of content, no matter how cheesey the dialogue. A mechanical robot with a computer brain is helped by the wizard Merlin to overcome the evil forces encroaching on the earth. See Picture below.

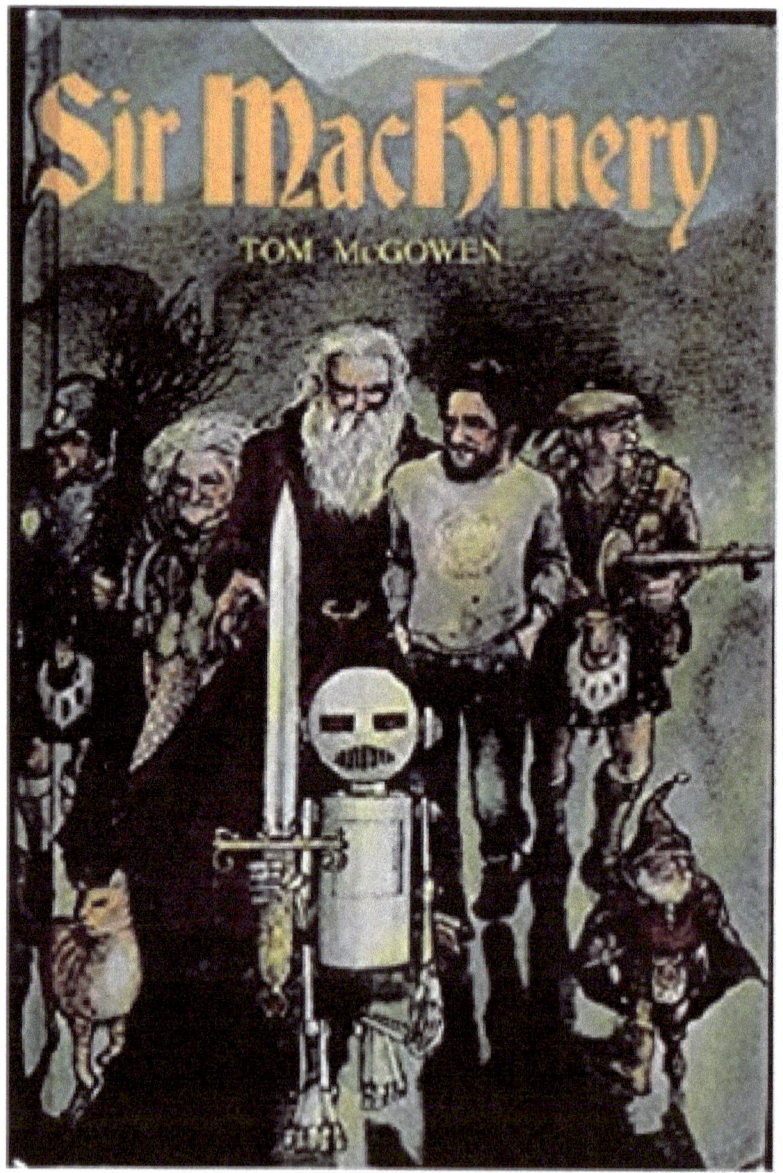

3. The Case for Marriage: Why Married couples are Happier,Healthier, Financial better off: a great book on the statistics on marriage versus widowed, single, divorced, cohabitating.

4. The Price of Leadership: actually a transcribed speech thatencapsulates many leadership traits I

believe work well.

5. Rich Dad, Poor Dad: great reading about the basics of business.

6. From Mosquitoes to Wolves: the history and evolution ofForward Air Control in Vietnam.

7. Officers in Flight Suits: six short stories of six Korean Warpilots that helps explain why different types of Air Force pilots are treated differently.

8. The Forgotten Man: a history of 1920s, 30s and 40s, critiquingheavily FDR (Roosevelt) and his administration.

9. The Roosevelt Myth: written in the 1940s and explains manyof the corrupt things the government had done for many years.

10. WW1 and WW2: both books were written by a British War

College professor and is a 40,000 foot view of the logistics of the Wars and how WW1 caused WW2.

What memory stands out the most from your military career?

What stands out the most to me about my military career was how God weaved my assignments together in a way to guide my military experiences and career that has prepared me to be where I am today.

God allowed me to have a desire to be a pilot and placed people around me to guide me throughout my careers. God allowed me to not get accepted into Warrant Officer Pilot Training right out of high school because I would have been a very immature officer. Spending a year enlisted and learning to be an aircraft mechanic has paid me dividends throughout my 40 year aviation career because because it grounded me and gave me a way to have something in common with all the mechanics I have worked with and they don't look at me as just some pilot who hadn't earned his way to be a pilot and thought mechanics were below their elevated status.

God orchestrated my assignment to Ft Lewis, WA versus Ft Campbell, KY which allowed me to apply for and attend WOFT a year early. He allowed me to be put in a WOFT class with older men who became my life long friends and mentors. I originally wanted to fly the UH-60 Blackhawk but God set men around me who convinced me that being an AH-1 Cobra pilot would be much better way to go. That decision has opened many more doors for me. All 4 UH-60 slots in our class went to Panama which didn't have an Embry-Riddle University campus to get a degree and all 4 slots were for a 4 year term so I would not have had my bachelors degree completed to be able to go to the Air Force or Navy and I would not have met Pam in NC. (ADDED: God's hand was protecting me by sending me to Ft Rucker for WOFT one month before the UH-60 I was responsible for and flew on crashed in a NVG training accident and killed all 4 on board).

God's hand in sending me to Camp LaGuardia, ROK and flying in the 4/7th Air Cavalry allowed me the opportunity to became an AH-1 Cobra Pilot in Command 18 months sooner than if had I been stationed anywhere else and allowed me to take CLEP tests toward my Bachelors degree. God stopping me from extending 6 months in Korea allowed me to meet Pam and begin taking college classes at Ft Bragg and finishing up before we got married.

All my Army training and experience allowed me a much better chance of becoming an AF or Navy pilot and allowed me to do extremely well in AF pilot training and help my classmates do well also. My experience as a Cobra pilot made becoming an F-16 Fighter pilot easier and again made me a better Fighter pilot and officer.

My Army experience and F-16 experience made me a much better ALO/FAC and allowed me to make my ALO unit a much better place by using that experience to build and run training opportunities that the ALOs could not. All my Army, fighter pilot, parachutist and ALO experience made me an easy choice to oversee the Close Air Support side of the planned Combat Parachute assault into Haiti.

God narrowed down the places I could get assigned

to after my ALO tour and we chose F-15Es to RAF Lakenheath, UK. This assignment allowed us the opportunity to go overseas and our family to live in a British neighborhood and the boys attend a local British school and our family to attend a wonderful church. All my previous experience made me the perfect person to be the Chief of Wing training at Lakenheath because one of the many things I had to accomplish was to write a Close Air Support training program and teach fellow F-15E aircrews to successfully accomplish that mission in Northern Iraq.

Our move to Columbus AFB, MS to teach in the T-37 was unexpected but I can see how God used it to allow me to help guide pilot students to become fighter pilots and surrounded me with pilots who educated me on what being an Airline Pilot would be like. I also was able to meet current SWA senior pilots who encourage me to apply there. My time as a T-37 Instructor made becoming Initial Cadre in the AF newest trainer the T-6A an easy transition and later made me a good Check Airman here at Southwest Airlines.

When I retired from active duty and joined the NC Air National Guard all my Army, fighter, ALO, and trainer experience helped me to mold, mentor and prepare this fledgling ALO unit into a Combat fighting force that has deployed several times to different combat zones.

Bottom line: what stands out most isn't what I did during my military career, but how God weaved it all together to make me who I am with the many many different experiences that allow me to train, mentor and evaluate thousands of SWA pilots from many different backgrounds. I can truly say: "Been there, Done that, Got that T-shirt".

Here are favorite memories that will forever be in my mind.

1. Meeting and marring my beautiful wife Pam, and having amilitary flare and sword detail in our wedding.

2. The birth of our oldest son, Daniel, in Fayetteville, NC and onlygetting to spend a couple of days after with Pam and Daniel before having deploy to the field (Prior to me, all other pilots got at least a week off; I got 2 days).

3. Thelossofourdaughter,Theodosia,atapproximately 6 months into Pam's pregnancy while I was in AF pilot training.

4. The birth of our second son, Andrew, at MacDill AFB at thebeginning of Operation Desert Shield (Iraq's invasion of Kuwait). The hospital was manned bare bones because a good portion of the hospital staff was deployed so Pam had little medical staff help.

5. The birth of our son, Turner, in Fayetteville, NC. I went on aweek long exercise 2 days after he was born because(I was stupid) I had organized a huge exercise at Ft Pickett, VA. That was the first of hundreds we were to accomplish and I felt I needed to make sure this first on was completed successfully.

Here are memories that stand out at each unit I was in.

1. Ft Lewis: The first time I flew on my assigned aircraft. Onemonth after I left for WOFT that aircraft was involved in an NVG training accident that destroyed the UH-60 and killed all 4 on board (I could have been one of them).

2. Ft Rucker: Having my family at my graduation.

3. Camp LaGuardia, ROK, 4/7th Air Cavalry: The first time I flewas the Pilot in Command. It was an NVG mission and while landing to get refueled we

encountered a Brown Out (Dust cloud from the Rotor wash) and had to go-around and try it again.

4. Ft Bragg, NC: Meeting Pam and flying a Cobra to Topsail Beachto try to find Pam on the beach and impress her. Then later flying a Cobra to Greenville, NC airport and having Pam meet me there so I could show her I was a cool pilot for real.

5. Homestead AFB: Evacuating for Hurricane Andrew.

6. Pope AFB/Ft Bragg, NC: Leading 120 AF officers and enlistedmen as we supported the 82nd Airborne Division on a combat parachute assault into Haiti (All the planning and meetings and preparation and loading 3,000+ airborne troops and equipment is unforgettable).

7. RAF Lakenheath: Flying missions of Northern Iraq.

8. Columbus AFB: Helping new pilots learn to fly and sendingthem out solo in an aircraft.

9. Moody AFB: Picking up 4 brand new T-6A Texans from thefactory.

10. Air National Guard: Deploying to Iraq and being there fortheir first election.

What would you say to someone considering joining the military?

F irst thing I would say, like I say to many things: Don't give me ten reasons NOT to do something; give me one reason that's legal and moral and do it.

My parents told us kids: Join the military, see the outside world (anything out of Nebraska), and if you don't like it you can always come back.

I have always been a proponent of doing something that might not be the easiest and safest thing to do when you are young because it will be harder to do it as you go older and have a wife and kids. An example of this was a SWA pilot I knew whose son was a West Point cadet. The dad asked me to talk his son into going aviation versus going Special Forces. I told the dad, it would be easier for him to go Special Forces and then become a pilot versus becoming a pilot then trying to go Special Forces.

I believe joining the military is alway a good option as long as the person choosing it has some basic ideas understood. 1. Once you actually swear in to leave for initial training you a locked into the next 3-6 years (depending on commitment). 2. It is going to be long days of training and you will get homesick but can't go home. 3. You have to spend lots of time away from loved ones, especially if you get stationed all the way across the US or on the other side of world. 4. The military does a lot of stupid stuff and treats people like cattle (lots of hurry up and wait. Example: show up 4 hours before your transportation leaves because they don't trust you). But this has be going on from the first day there ever was a military. I tell people that the military generals really want to take good care of their people. Problem is there are thousands of intermediate leaders that have their own agenda (or are just stupid) and make everything painful.

I believe the military has a lot of great training to offer and if you work hard you can get promoted and get more great training. The military also gets to do a lot of fun things like shooting guns and rockets, dropping bombs, parachuting, scuba diving, and flying aircraft. Military training can prepare you for jobs like flying, welding, fixing vehicles and aircraft and air conditioning and it is all free (sort of). I tell everyone that NOTHING is FREE: You either pay for it with your wallet (money) or with your body (3-6 year commitment of your life). But the military is the only place that has jobs that only military can have and if you want to be a special operator, attack helicopter pilot or fighter pilot you can't do it in the civilian world.

I've been told and I believe it. That the first two years of College is to get you out on your own and the last two years you actually learn something. A three year enlistment is about the same. The only difference is that you can't come home on weekends.

Having been on active duty and in the National Guard what I would ask my grand children or anyone else is what do you hope to do 10 years from now? How do you plan to pay for the training/education you need?

If someone doesn't know the answer to these two

questions other than "I don't want to be away from loved one or I don't mind moving away" then I would say (If they don't mind moving) enlist into a service for a job you think you might enjoy or something that will be really cool to tell your kids and grandkids someday. Do it for a tour. Mature and use the GI-Bill to get a degree in something that you now understand you will like and something that you can support your family with. (If don't want to move away) Join the National Guard, pick a job that you think would give you the training to lead to a good civilian job or pick a cool job (example: tank driver) that you can brag about while you are at UNC or NC State taking classes that are being paid for by the National Guard. You will have to be gone for initial training for at least 6 months and maybe one deployment, but on average just one weekend a month and 2 weeks in the summer.

Turner once asked me if my military training taught how to get multiple things done and did it make me who I was. I said "No, all the military did was give me NON-Normal opportunities (some really cool but dangerous) to hone my abilities and attributes. Had I gone right to college and became a systems analyst or accountant or lawyer I would have been one with the same attributes of busy and multi-tasking. Actually I could not have gone to college following HS because I did so poorly in school, but that's beside the point. My parents quit parenting after kid number 10, Haha. But the military didn't didn't care about my past poor performance in academics. They liked my current test scores and work ethic and physical fitness. Also I didn't say Doctor because I don't like hospitals because there are sick people there and I don't have much empathy for people and wouldn't have a good bedside manner. I would probably just yell at them to get UP, quit whining, get well, NOW, DO IT.

So Bottom line what would I tell someone who is

considering the military:

I would say go for it, but understand your reasoning why and understand all the options and that everyone's experience is different. God didn't make the perfect job, God made you to make each job you do perfect (from the "Price of Leadership"}. Then I would find two different people in each job the person is looking at to talk to so they have the best idea what they are getting into as possible.

What have been your worst injuries?

I will answer this question in two ways: 1 - Physical injuries and 2 - Mental injuries

Physical injuries:

1. I would say my worst physical injury was my run in with alarge work van last year down in Fayetteville, NC in front of the abortion clinic. I got hit by a speeding van's passenger side mirror in the middle of my right side chest area, breaking 4 ribs. I was also thrown into nearby bushes which cut up my face and arms. I was out of work for 2 months.

2. Out of 115 Static-line Parachute jumps, I had 2 less thanperfect landing and twisted my right ankle both times. I didn't miss work but I certainly limped for a few days.

3. I was involved in a small plane accident and during the crashmy left leg just above the ankle hit a bolt and cut my leg. I also had a sore back for about a week.

4. While in Korea and during a Martial Arts (Hap Kido) practice Itwisted my right ankle doing a jumping spinning kick and came down hard on it while still spinning.

5. When I was 14 I was fooling around with some blank 7.62mmcasings. One of the primers of one of the casing was set off and shot straight down into my right foot and lodged under my skin and had to be removed by a doctor. It also bruised my foot for a few days.

6. At age 12 I was kicked in the teeth by a cow and my top twofront teeth were knocked loose. After a few weeks they became solid again.

7. As a 5 year old while we were picking up and loading hay balesI fell off the front of the trailer and my legs were run over by one of the wheels of trailer. I can't remember if it hurt or not, but I know the grass cushioned the weight of the trailer and my Dad yelled at me to get up and get back on the trailer, so I did.

Mental injuries:

1. I believe a mental injury that affected me the most was as a 5thgrader. My brother Mark and I were way behind during our 6th and 4th grade years respectfully so our parents in an effort to help us catch up had us repeat those grade but at a different school (Hebron vs Meridian). They had to pay $2,000 for each of us to go to Hebron (lots of money 50 years ago. College tuition was only $700 a year) so I know they only wanted the best for us (and to save on taxes they paid me and Mark each $2,000 for farm work, and Mark and I would each write a check to Hebron to pay for our own tuition). After our first year in Hebron my parents made a deal with the Hebron school district for Mark, me, David, JoAnne, and Rhonda to attend Hebron also because they saw it was a much better school. The deal was the cost for Mark and I would continue to be $2,000 a year each but David, JoAnne, and Rhonda would only have

to pay $100 each. So now that you know this, I will explain my mental injury. During my 5th grade year Mark and I still were not doing as well as my mother had hoped and (I now believe out of desperation) my mother tried to get Mark and I to work harder said "Why can't you be more like David and do better in school? We are paying $2,000 each a year for you to go to Hebron and you are wasting it!" WOW that hurt (I didn't say it, But...) my first thought was, well why don't you have David pay $2,000 for school and I can just pay $100. I spent pretty much most of the rest of my Mom's life trying to prove to her I was just as smart as David and envied David. In 1997 after my mom's and her sisters visit to England to see us, I finally realized I didn't need to prove anything to her and I had never needed to envy David (Lots of wasted mental anguish, but it did drive me to do many of the things I have accomplished, but kind of for the wrong reasons). I can't wait to get to Heaven and hug her and thank her.

2. As a dumb 16 year old, the morning my Dad died I had a not sogood interaction with my Dad in our greenhouse and as I was walking out I said to myself "I wish you would just get out of my life." Four hours later I was informed at school that he had a heart attack and died and was "out of my life" now. I have regretted that morning everyday of my life and wish I hadn't said that but I did. Rarely a week goes by that I don't wish he had lived for me to have been able to ask for his guidance or meet my children. He never came to one of my sports event (he did come to a couple of band concerts). He did show me in his actions that God and going to church were important and how to act like a man and how to treat women in a good way. Since I never got to have him go to most of the sports and big events in my life I have probably overcompensated and tried to attend every

event I could of my kids and grandkids. I can't wait to get to Heaven and hug him and thank him.

3.   The loss of our daughter Theodosia was hard on me mentally.Pam got very sick and hemorrhaged a massive amount of blood and I was afraid she would die also. A day doesn't go by that I don't think about her and wonder what it would have been like to have to let her date and know that I wasn't able to walk her down the aisle in marriage. I wonder what her kids would have been like, but God has blessed me with grand daughters and this has allowed me to see and experience, in a small part, what I missed not being able to raise her. I do long for the day that I get to Heaven and hold her in my arms and tell her face to face I have loved her and missed her. I do believe Pam's sister Susan cradled her in her arms when God took her to Heaven and showed her the love we were unable to do. I also believe my Mom, Dad, Aunt Pat, Grandpa and Grandma DeWald have shown her how to play "Down on the Farm" and 10 point Pitch. And my Dad's parents and sisters have shown her how to dance to and sing Polka music.

Who have been the most spiritually influential people in your life?

※◇◇◇◇◇◇◇◇◇◇◇◇※

Following are people who helped me understand that Jesus is who He claimed to be, that He was born of a virgin, lived a sinless life, suffered and died on the cross for our sins, and was raised from the dead 3 days later.

My dad, Charles M. Votipka, helped me understand how important going to church and serving God was to him. His example showed me that it was manly to follow Jesus and to ensure one's family gets to church and serve God in our daily lives.

My mom, Fern J. Votipka, helped me understand that serving God by teaching children His truths and the importance of attending regular church services.

My grandparents, Ralph Oscar (RO) and Ferne DeWald, helped me understand that belief in God and serving Him was important to raise a large family and run a very successful large scale farm.

My wife, Pamela F. Votipka, helped me understand the importance of reading and understanding the Bible (God's Holy Word) and praying for and serving other less fortunate.

My in-laws, John and Sylvia Fisher, helped me understand the importance of following God in all aspects of one's life and the importance of serving in your church.

Our pastor at East End Baptist Church in Columbus MS, Brother Jerry, helped me understand how we should not be a stumbling block to others, especially my children, in coming to know Jesus as their Lord and Savior.

My children, Daniel, Andrew, and Turner, have shown me how that by following and serving God from an early age that a person's life can be filled with all the wonderful blessings God has prepared for us and that His grace is sufficient for our lives.

Where did you go to church growing up? What do you remember most about it?

My family and I attended St. Mary's Catholic Church in Alexandria, Nebraska, which was three miles from our house. It was two miles as the crow flies, so attending an 8:30am church service only required us to have to leave the house by 8:20. But we always left our house at 8am. It's the church my mother grew up in and my Grandpa and Grandma DeWald lived in the house across the street where this picture was taken.

What I remember most was serving as an altar boy and ringing the large bell that was located on the backside of the church. We took turns ringing it and because it was so large it would actually lift you off the ground as you pulled and held the rope as it swung the bell side to side. We had so many young boys we could have as many as ten altar Boys every Sunday. You could become an altar boy after First Communion and you could serve for several years until you were in high school and old enough to be in the choir. I also remember my Uncle Phillip and Aunt Dixie and their family of ten alway sat in the front left pew and my parents and our family sat right behind them. Usually there weren't more than my mom and dad and kids under 7 because the rest were either altar boys or in the Choir or no longer at home. The Church has a large basement that was a large hall for events and Catechism up to the 5th Grade.

St. Mary's Catholic Church, Alexandria, Nebraska

The Bell at St. Mary's Catholic Church, Alexandria, Nebraska

In the summer of 1980, after my dad passed away in January my brother Mark left for the Army after graduating from high school. My mom and sister Rhonda and I moved to a house my mom purchased across the street from Sacred Heart Catholic Church in Hebron, NE.

What I remember most was that Sacred Heart had a daily morning Mass and that boys served as altar boys until they graduated from high school. Girls sang in the choir through high school also. Since there was daily Mass, Saturday evening Mass, and Sunday morning Mass we didn't serve as altar boys every Sunday, but a schedule was set up for each service which meant you served morning daily Mass once every 2 weeks and Saturday or Sunday Mass once a month.

I also remember that we had Catechism on Wednesday nights and we went all the away through 12th grade. St Mary's had Catechism on Saturday mornings and we only went through the 6th grade because all the families were farmers and we were needed to work on Saturdays.

I remember that it was impressive that at Sacred Heart the altar was positioned so that the priest looked out on the congregation as he did Mass as opposed to St Mary's where the priest's back was to the congregation.

Sacred Heart Catholic Church in Hebron, Nebraska. We lived across the street just left of the church in this picture.

What was your dream car?

Over the years my dream car has changed.

Originally it was a 1956 Chevy all hopped up as a muscle car.

Then it was an MG Midget or an Austin Healey Sprite English Sports car. (I did fix up a 67 Austin Healey Sprite in high school)

Austin Healey Sprite

Then it was a Porsche 911 Targa

Then I dreamed of owning a 10 cylinder engine Jaguar
XKE

Then my senior year in high school my brother Mark was getting stationed in Germany and left me his 1966 Ford Mustang. It didn't have a muscle car V8 engine, only an in-line 6 cylinder engine with a 3 speed manual transmission. It wasn't fast but it was neat to drive.

As I was getting ready to graduate from high school and hoping to be a military pilot someday I knew I needed to own a sports car. So at my first duty station at Ft Lewis, WA I bought a 1969 Camaro. It was cool and didn't have seat belts and I didn't have to have insurance.

When I got to Army pilot training I realized if I was going to continue to send money home to help my mother I couldn't afford a Porsche or Jaguar, especially when I finally realized we really didn't get paid much as a Warrant Officer trainee and a Warrant Officer. Once I subtracted taxes, food, housing, gas, and sending 25% of my pay to help my mother, all that was left was enough to buy a 1974 VW Diesel Rabbit. It got 40 miles to the gallon and was kind of sporty.

When I returned from Korea I bought a Datsun 280Z. It was like a Jaguar XKE but very cheap. It looked cool and was fast.

Then I got married and started to have kids and I really realized that a car was just mode of transportation. So it was mini-vans for me and Pam.

So bottom line: My car would be............... A 1969, 10 Cylinder engined Jaguar XKE.

What school(s) did you go to growing up? What do you remember most about school?

We were in the Meridian School District, and it was divided into 3 different school locations. You attended kindergarten at the school nearest you. Grades 1-3 were in Daykin (about 10 miles from our farm). Grades 4-6 were at Alexandria (3 miles from our farm). Junior High (7-8th grades) and High School (9-12th grades) were in Tobias (about 15 miles from our farm). The bus system went like this: Your local bus picked you up and took you to your local school building where you lived (in our case, Alexandria). Then if you were going to Daykin or Tobias you would stay on and go to Daykin. In Daykin, the junior and senior high students from Alexandria and Daykin would get on the Tobias bus and the grades 4-6 from Tobias and Daykin would get on the Alexandria bus.

I attended kindergarten at Alexandria Elementary School, Alexandria, NE. What I remember most was that it was half-day. I rode the bus to school, and someone picked me up after lunch, and we had a nap time. I also remember that two of my cousins (Tracy and Jackie DeWald) were in my class and both could read already. I had just turned 5 and they both were almost 6.

I attended grades 1-3 at the Daykin Elementary School, Daykin, NE. What I remember most about it was that it had an awesome monkey bars and swing set, and it had a large gravel play yard and grass covered baseball field. It had an auditorium/gym and kitchen/lunchroom where we got our lunch from and where we did PE in the cold and rainy days. We had 15 minutes recess in the morning and afternoon and an hour for lunch and recess. I remember once the Norris Power company came with an educational van and talked to us about nuclear power and how it was so much better than coal. I also remember an acting troop from some big city came and had us kind of audition to be extras to perform in a play they were putting on at the school that evening. I was selected and my parents brought me back that evening to see the play. Looking back and remembering that this was in 1970 (my sister Kathy and brother Tom were in Vietnam) I believe this acting troop were some what we would now call hippies. The play, as best I can remember was about how litter and trash were destroying the Earth (I had not been to a fast food place at this time). Looking back, I don't think any of the parents enjoyed the play and that is probably why the acting troop got kids to be part of the play so that adults would attend.

I attended 4th grade back in Alexandria, so I only had to ride one bus and since we had to wait for the bus to come from Daykin, we got to play in the school playground while we waited. The school had an attached auditorium/ gym and kitchen/lunchroom, a football field, and baseball diamond. Our recess and lunch schedule was the same as we had in grades 1-3 and I remember a few times I was kept from recess for getting into trouble in class.

I next attended Hebron Elementary in Hebron, NE and

repeated the 4th grade because my parents felt I didn't do well enough in Meridian school system. They were going to allow me to move up to the 5th grade but my parents didn't feel I should have. They were right. Having been a summer baby and number 12 of 13 kids, I was well behind my classmates and I probably would have stayed behind for several years. What I remember most about 4-6th grade at Hebron Elementary is that the 3 story building had a fire escape tube that you got to slide down during fire drills.

I next attended Hebron Junior/Senior High, also in Hebron, NE. What I remember most was the great teachers in all the grades and the very large Vocational Training building. In half of the building we had a ten bay auto mechanics shop and the other half was divided into a welding shop and a wood working shop. I remember many good teachers that I still quote today for some of their wise sayings. I especially remember Mr. Goodrich. He was a 22 year Air Force aircraft mechanic who taught us Auto Mechanics and really help ground us in doing good work and learning how to troubleshoot car problems. He had a photo development lab in his house basement and used to teach some of us how to develop black and white photos. I also remember that because the average class size was 40, students interested in athletics could go out for a sport and make the team because they were needed to fill up the team slots.

After high school, I went to night school with Embry-Riddle Aeronautical University at the Ft Bragg International campus for my Bachelors degree. What I remember most was that I was able to take two classes each night on Monday/Wednesday and Tuesday/Thursday, with the first class from 5:30-7:30pm and a second class from 8:00-10:00pm. So after working a full 8 hour day we spent 4 hours in school each night and doing homework during the weekends. There were some classes at 8am - 4pm on Saturdays. Sometimes I would finish class at 10pm during the week then going to the airfield and flying a 4 hour training mission from 10:30pm to 2:30am.

At RAF Lakenheath I went to Night School with Embry-Riddle Aeronautical University International campus for my Master's degree. What I remember most was it was a lot more work having to write lots of papers and speeches. But having my Master's allowed me to teach Bachelor's and Master's classes for Embry-Riddle the next 5 years of my military career.

Where was your favorite place that you lived in (other than Rocky Mount!)?

I would have to say Columbus AFB, MS.

Why do I say this? Because in many ways it was like living the way I grew up. It was safe for the boys to go to the bowling alley and golf course on their own. All the neighbors watched out for others kids and everyone knew each other and was polite. I was home pretty much every night and got to be involved in all the activities at school, sports, and church. East End Baptist Church was filled with godly people and everyone wanted to minister to the neighborhood and each other. The boys' school was very good and provided lots of opportunities for them.

Living at Columbus AFB was as close to what life was like back in the Beaver Cleaver days and what I believe life was like in the 1950s.

RAF Lakenheath assignment and living in Great Hockham, UK was my next favorite because of the all the many benefits it had for Pam and the boys.

Did you know any of your grandparents? What were they like?

I did not know my Dad's parents very well since they passed away when I was around 5 years old. What I know about them is that my Grandma Votipka was a very hard working woman who ran their farm and household. My Grandpa Votipka was a typical Bohemian father for those days and was not a hands on father to his children.

As for my Grandpa and Grandma DeWald, I had the opportunity to know them and spend time with them. My Grandpa RO DeWald was 6 feet tall and was as an imposing man who loved God, his wife, his children, and his church. He, with Grandma DeWald, were able to be very successful during the Great Depression and ended up owning many farms and acres of land that he used to give his children a great start on life and help others in the county. Grandpa DeWald was known for lending money to help people start farms and businesses who couldn't get loans from the banks, and all with just the shake of a hand. He lived his motto: People will not be trustworthy if you don't trust them. Grandpa DeWald lived his faith in Jesus Christ and sometimes to a fault demanded others (especially his children) do the same. It would not be uncommon for him to notice you weren't in church and call you afterwords to find out why you weren't there. (He never retired from farming but moved off the farm to a house across the street from church). Grandpa DeWald never had a problem letting you know what he thought and what he believed you should think also. He loved having his children and grandchildren around him and enjoyed having us over to their house to play cards (10 point Pitch, Down on the Farm,...). Even though he was a big man, he was a wonderful model of how a man should treat his wife and family.

As for Grandma Ferne DeWald, she was 5 feet tall and was just as imposing as Grandpa and when she talked, he listened. She was the oldest of 10 children. She overcame Polio at age ten and went on to play girls basketball in high school, and helped her husband build a large successful farm and raise 10 children of her own. Grandma loved God, her husband, her children and grandchildren, and her local community. She was ahead of her time as a young woman and ran the Hebron, NE Post Office when she was 18-21 (her Dad was working their also and Grandma had to take up his slack when he traveled to play the violin in different states). Grandpa DeWald had asked her to marry him when she was 19 but told him she would not get married until she was 21 and had turned the Post Office over to someone else to run it. Grandma was a great record keeper and documented everything. She was as sharp as a tack until the day she died at 96 from bone cancer. She could name every one of her 80 grandkids and 150 great grandkids and was well read and could talk about the most current events at age 96. She was a wonderful example of what to expect from a wife, mother, and grandmother. She loved having us to her house and playing cards and treating us to home made candies.

Who are the funniest people in your family?

Wow that is a very interesting question. My immediate family was way too serious about most things and I don't remember any of my siblings being funny.

If funny means doing pranks, I believe Pam's brother JT would take the prize for that and my sons Andrew and Turner would be a close second to JT.

As far as someone being the funniest I would have to say my son Andrew with Turner being a close second. Andrew's humor sometimes can be dry but he has some great ways to make people laugh. Turner's humor is his directness and shirtlessness when he wants to shock people or just have fun.

When was the first time you left Nebraska?

The first time left the state of Nebraska (even though I only lived 12 miles North of Kansas) was in 1972 when my brother Tom got married in Oklahoma City, OK.

The next time I left Nebraska was in May 1980 when we traveled to the US Air Force Academy in Colorado Springs, CO for my brother David's graduation.

The next time was when I flew to San Antonio, TX for my brother David's graduation from Air Force Pilot training in Del Rio, TX in June of 1981.

Then in August of 1981, I traveled across the border from Omaha, NE to Council Bluffs, IA to take the Military Entrance Tests and Aviation Test. Then a year later I left Nebraska to go to Ft Jackson in Columbia, South Carolina for Army Basic Training.

Why did you join the military?

Wow, what a great question for which there are a few answers.

It would be easy to just say it was a family tradition but that would be just the tip of the iceberg.

Yes, 9 of my siblings joined the military and my parents we very proud of them and my siblings that did not join the military. My Dad, who served in combat in World War II, said many times "Join the military and see the world and if you want to continue to live out in the big world do so, you will always have a place back here if you want to come back."

Forty+ years ago, college was cheap enough that you could work during the summers and earn enough to pay for tuition and then have a job during college to pay for room and board. Student loans were not necessary (I don't know if they even existed).

Typically less than 20% of a graduating high school class went to college. Most went to a trade school or right into a job and you could work your way to the top. Joining the military would give a person a skill and training and money for college when they got out (all my siblings used their eduction benefits, GI Bill, to get college degrees and other training).

To be honest, I didn't do well in school and graduated with basically a C+ average, so I doubt I could have gotten directly into college even if I had wanted to do so. But since I wanted to be a pilot from the age of 12 and no desire (nor ability) to get an ROTC scholarship and had no chance to be accepted into a Military Academy, I had to figure out a way to learn to fly since I didn't have any money to pay for flying lessons. My brothers-in-law, Roger Retzlaff and Byron Bond, had told me stories of Army Warrant Officer helicopter pilots flying them into combat in Vietnam. I saw that as an opportunity. Then my sister JoAnne joined the Army as a Helicopter mechanic and wanted to become a pilot through Warrant Officer pilot training. I started to look in that direction since a college degree wasn't needed.

My original plan was to learn to fly in the Army for 4 years and come back to Nebraska and become a Crop Duster and start my own crop dusting business. When my brother David went through Air Force pilot training and I saw military jets at airshows, I thought that would be something I could do after getting my degree that the military would pay for and it would be great to be a helicopter pilot while I got my degree.

A big factor in wanting to join the military was that the Cold War was raging and I had a desire to defend our country just like my Dad and siblings who served in Vietnam. I had watched many war movies and thought it would be cool to get away from the little farm and see the world and stand up against the evil Soviet Union. I had alway thought (and still do today) that someone needs to be ready to defend my friends and family and fellow Americans, so why not me.

So bottom line, why did I join? I wanted to fight Communism and the evil empire, I wanted to be a pilot and fly combat missions and do really cool things and blow stuff up, I knew I wasn't ready to go straight into college (plus I knew I wouldn't get in), I didn't have any money and the military would pay for all my training, and joining had become a family tradition. I was hoping there was a beautiful red head out there somewhere that I could impress and get her to marry me (I had actually dreamt that in my 11th grade year).

I thought as a minimum: Enlist in, learn how to fix aircraft and if I didn't get into Flight training I would come back to Nebraska and use my GI Bill benefits to attend college and become an accountant or computer systems analyst while I worked on aircraft and learned to fly on my own. I definitely had no desire to make it a career since I only knew one person who had been in the military long enough to retire and he never recommended a 20 year military career. Once I started flying in the military I was enjoying the many cool and dangerous things I got to do and got addicted to the thrill of risks (plus I ended up owing 4 years for Army pilot Training and 8 years for Air Force pilot training so I had almost 17 years in before I could have thought to get out).

God had a plan for me to meet and marry that BEAUTIFUL RED HEAD and at the same time be ready to defend out great nation against the Communist hordes. And having fun (most of the time) while doing so in the military was the path that gave me all those options.

What things from home did you miss the most while you were serving in the military?

I have to split this answer into two different times: "Before I Married Pam" and "After I Married Pam".

Before: When I was initially in the military and before I married Pam, I don't remember missing being in Nebraska and being around family and friends because I was having fun meeting new people and seeing new things. But after a couple of years I missed the seeing and visiting with my family (but I did get to spend time with my sister Cynthia and her family in South Carolina and sister Nancy and her family in Oregon). Even though I made new friends, I missed doing things with my friend Greg Bodtke, brother Mark and friend Jeff Retzlaff. I missed playing cards with my mother and grand parents and playing football at Thanksgiving with my cousins from the Hergott family. I missed being able to go hunting on our farm without having to get a license or ask permission of any farmer.

After: When I got married to Pam and we started to have children, what I missed changed tremendously. When I deployed I would now miss Pam and playing with Daniel, Andrew, and Turner. I missed being there for their birthdays and Thanksgiving and Christmas. I missed not being able to go to Church with them and go to their sporting events and band concerts. I missed not being able to attend church events with them and help in AWANAs or RAs.

Basically once I got married, my life revolved around those who were with me where the military moved me.

Tell me what a typical day in the military was like for you.

There were truly nine distinct phases or different lives I lived during my time in on active duty in the military. Basic Training, UH-60 crewchief, Army pilot training, attack helicopter pilot, Air Force pilot training, F-16 pilot, Air Liaison Officer/Forward Air Controller, F-15E pilot, and finally T-37/T-6A instructor.

Army Basic Training days (the days were long but the weeks were short):

5:30am wake up and dress for physical fitness training and completed by 6:30am
6:30am quick shower and go to Dining Facility by 7am
7:30am line up to start morning training (Weapons training, marching training, ...)
12 noon break for lunch

1:00pm line up for the afternoon training (Chemical warfare training, map reading, hand grenade training....)
5:00pm break for dinner
5:30pm clean weapons and the barracks or the unit outside area prepare uniform for the next day
9:00pm lights out

My time at Ft Lewis, WA as a UH-60 crew chief days

6:30am quick shower and go to Dining Facility by 7am (no requirement to eat breakfast)
7:30am report to aircraft hanger to get assigned work for the day (fixing and preparing UH-60s for missions)
12 noon break for lunch
1:00pm
4:00pm break for physical fitness training (Mondays, Wednesdays. Fridays)
5:00pm eat supper
6:00pm attend night school or fly night missions

My time at Ft Rucker, AL for Army pilot training
6:30am quick shower and go to Dining Facility by 7am
7:30am report to aircraft hangars to fly training flights
12 noon break for lunch
1:00pm attend flight training academic classes
4:00pm break for physical fitness training (Mondays, Wednesdays. Fridays)
5:00pm eat supper
6:00pm study and prepare for class the next day

My time in Korea and Ft Bragg, NC
6:00am Physical fitness training (Mondays. Wednesdays, Fridays)
7:30am report to aircraft hangars to fly training flights or prepare for training flights
12 noon break for lunch
1:00pm report to aircraft hangars to fly training flights or prepare for training flights
6:00pm attend night school or fly night missions

My time at Vance AFB, OK for Air Force Pilot training
6:30am report to aircraft hangars to fly training flights
12 noon break for lunch
1:00pm attend flight training academic classes
4:00pm break for physical fitness training (Mondays, Wednesdays. Fridays)
6:00pm study and prepare for class the next day

My time at Homestead AFB, FL and RAF Lakenheath England flying the F-16 and F-15E and Columbus AFB, and Moody AFB
7:30am report to Fighter Squadrons to fly training flights or prepare for training flights
12 noon break for lunch (usually went to gym to work out)
1:00pm report to aircraft hangers to fly training flights or prepare for training flights
6:00pm attend Night School (Masters classes) or Fly night missions

My time at Pope AFB, NC as and ALO/FAC
7:30am Physical Fitness training (Mondays, Wednesdays. Fridays)
9:00am report to Squadron to do CAS training or prepare for training missions and parachute operations
12 noon break for lunch
1:00pm report to Squadron to do CAS training or prepare for training missions and parachute operations
6:00pm attend Night School (Masters classes) or do night CAS and parachute missions

How do you feel your time in the military changed you as a person?

Wow, this is a tough question.

I don't think the military changed me a lot as a person but what it did was allow me to excel in the areas I was good at (hard work, physical fitness, hand-eye-coordination). I will admit that probably the one area I was changed was that I was surrounded by many more experienced combat veterans who helped mature my self important attitude by letting me know that no matter how smart or fast (running) or good my pilot skills were, there would always be someone smarter or faster or a better pilot than me. Once I understood that, instead of trying to brag about myself, I needed to just work hard at everything I did and support those around me in the training and missions we did. I learned that I needed to do any job I was given and not feel like anything was below me. As a small example of how this has paid me dividends even today, many pilots will not push wheelchair passengers onto the aircraft. But I will and it is recognized by the passengers and my coworkers.

Now I guess you could say the perspective of others about me changed because of my time in the military. As I said before, I didn't do extremely well in high school and many people in my family and school mates and teachers were surprised that I was able to become a military pilot and officer. The work ethic and physical fitness I acquired growing up on the farm was recognized by the military and I was selected and trained to be a military aviator.

What was one of the best parts about your time in the military?

I don't think I can narrow it down to one.

If I can only choose one, it would be the fact that I ended up stationed at Ft Bragg, NC and met and married the most beautiful and godly woman who had the grace and stamina to raise three wonderful boys and move to wherever I got stationed and made each place a home for all of us.

Now, since it is my book I will add on other things (they don't rival Pam, but were very good)

1. I got to take Daniel and Andrew on Close Air Support Trainingmissions at Ft. Pickett, VA. Daniel, Andrew and our dog Hart got to ride in my HUMMV with me from Ft Bragg to spend 3 days doing training at Ft Pickett.

2. I got to be a UH-60 Blackhawk crew chief at a very low rank and age.

3. I got to fly AH-1 Cobra helicopters at a young age and preparedto fight a war in Korea, Europe, Middle East, and South America if need be.

4. I got to fly F-16s and F-15Es

5. I got to make 115 static line parachute jumps and become aJump Master and Master Parachutist (I came within 2 weeks of getting to attend a secret HALO parachute school before it was cancelled due to funding).

6. I got to work with Army Rangers, Special Forces, RegularInfantry, Marines, Delta Force, and Navy Seals and train them to provide close air support in an emergency.

7. As Initial Cadre in the Air Force's new T-6A training, I got topickup and deliver 5 new aircraft from the factory to Moody AFB, GA. It's rare that a military pilot gets to double the flight time on an aircraft on one leg of a flight. I got to do it 5 times (the brand new planes had been test flown for <2.5 hours each. The flight to Moody was 3 hours).

8. I got to travel to many places in the world to do my job of supporting ground troops.

What was one of the most difficult experiences during your time in the military, and how did you get through it?

One of my most difficult experiences was when I was an Air Liaison Officer/Forward Air Controller (ALO/FAC) with the Detachment 1/507th Air Control Wing (which later became 14th Air Support Operations Squadron/18th Air Support Operations Group 14th ASOS/18th ASOG) while stationed at Ft Bragg/Pope AFB, NC October 1992 to June 1995.

So what was the experience? Why was it difficult? And how did I get through it?

In the spring of 1993, the 74th Fighter Squadron was starting to be formed alongside the two A-10 squadrons that had arrived in late summer of 1992 (75th and 76th Fighter Squadrons). This new squadron would be comprised of many of the F-16Cs I had flown at the recently destroyed Homestead AFB, FL. I thought this was going to be great because I thought that once my ALO/FAC tour was over in a year I would get re-qualified in the F-16C and stay another three years in Fayetteville for a total of five years at one base. As all three squadrons built up their pilot force and training flights it started to become apparent that many of the senior pilots in the A-10 and especially the F-16 squadrons in an effort to beef up their promotion resumes wanted to coordinate directly with the Army Infantry and Special Forces units we supported. The problem was that the Army side of our planning that ALOs did was completed over several months leading up to an actual mission that required jets to perform CAS missions. Since most fighter units only plan a day or two in advance for local Close Air Support (CAS) missions it would be nearly impossible for them to be coordinated directly together. That is why the ALO/FAC units were formed during WWII to bridge the gap between the Army and Air Force CAS missions and training. Not only did the senior A-10 and F-16 not understand this, but they truly didn't care and openly made disparaging remarks about our ALO/FAC unit and us as ALO/FACs. They constantly let us know they didn't need us and could do our job better than us.

Another thing they didn't understand was that they were the "New Kids on the Block." We had 50 years of processes and procedures formalized. The the 82nd that had been working very well with us and we had over 30 Fighter Squadrons that we had access to for training, ranging from A-10s and Navy A-4 in Pennsylvania, Air National Guard F-16s and Navy A-6s and F-14s in Virginia, Marine Harriers and AF F-15Es in North Carolina, and active duty and Air National Guard F-16s and active duty A-10s in South Carolina. So the coordination process was easy for our ALO/FAC unit. We would spend 2-3 months working on the Army's maneuver training plan and then a couple days prior we would call all thirty Fighter units and easily find 3-4 sets of fighters to work the exercise. The saddest thing about the new F-16 74th FS and these senior pilots was that they wanted to pad their promotion files but we were never able to get them to fly any of the local CAS missions. I even had one senior pilot tell me that CAS was not their job and it wasn't "cool" to do so they were avoiding the missions. This mentality really rubbed me raw and caused some unneeded tension between the 74th FS and the 14th ASOS.

So what was the difficult experience? In February 1994, near the end of the day, I received a phone call from one of the army battalions I supported. The commander asked me if I was going to be at the meeting the next day with his training planners and the two pilots from the A-10 and F-16 squadrons. I informed him I didn't know anything about it, but said thanks for letting me know and I would be there. The next morning I showed up at the Army units meeting room and the Army officers are there and they waved at me and said "Hi Opie." The two AF pilots, one was a major and the other was a captain like me. His last name was Duckworth. He looked sternly at me and said "Captain Votipka, what are you doing here?" And I said back to them "This is one of my units and the commander asked me to be here." Then the major said "Just sit in the corner over there. We can do this, we don't need you."

Why was it difficult? Well first off, AF pilots don't call each other by their rank, so in doing so they were telling me that I was less than they were. Secondly, this was done in front of one of my supported Army units and they actually had purposely gone behind my back to set up the meeting. My concern was that this was setting an unworkable precedent with fighter squadrons working directly with Army units because neither of them had authority to coordinate range air space and it was not realistic real world coordination for combat operations.

How did I get through it? After the meeting once the AF pilots left, I assured the Army commander that our ALO/FACs would continue to coordinate and provide the high quality training they were used to. I knew that the AF pilots had ZERO clue what they were getting into and sooner or later they would be in over their heads. Well it happened sooner rather than later. Within two weeks Lt. General Hugh Shelton (18th Airborne Corps Commander) had his staff contact the AF captain Duckworth and wanted him to meet with the General's staff and arrange future training events. Captain Duckworth called me and asked me to come with him because he was not sure what General Shelton's staff wanted, but Captain Duckworth was sure he could handle it himself. He just wanted me there just in case. So that day an Army UH-1 helicopter came to Pope AFB and picked us up and flew us to where General Shelton and his staff were in the field on an exercise. During the flight, Captain Duckworth kept telling me he was well prepared and really didn't need my help. I was laughing to myself because he really didn't have a clue how the Army operated and Shelton's colonels were going to eat his lunch. We arrived at the briefing room and Shelton's Chief of Staff, Colonel Nelson comes into the room and says "Hi Opie. How are you doing. I didn't know you were coming but glad you are here." Colonel Nelson then turns to Captain Duckworth and says "Captain Duckworth, are you ready to work with my staff today and set up training to the next 12 months?" Duckworth's eyes got real big and stutters back, "Uh, Sir, we don't operate like that and my general over at Pope AFB will not sign up for that long of a commitment." Colonel Nelson looked at him and said "I believe your One Star General will do whatever Three Star General Shelton tells him to do!" I almost started laughing out loud because I knew this was going to happen. Captain Duckworth who is now visibly shaken stutters back and said "I'm, I'm s-s-s-sorry sir, but, but I'm, I'm going to have to take this back to my boss." Colonel Nelson looked at him and said "Captain, today is Friday. By next Friday YOU WILL

HAVE SAT DOWN WITH MY STAFF AND COMPLETED A 12 MONTH CALENDAR. DO YOU UNDERSTAND ME!!!!" Poor Captain Duckworth looked like a scared child and said "Ah, Ah yes sir." Colonel Nelson turned and left the room and Duckworth and I started walking to the helicopter. I was trying to hold back from busting out laughing and Duckworth was trying to keep from crying.

On the flight home Captain Duckworth now addressed me as Opie and said "Hey Opie, can you help me figure this out?" I told him "Hey, first off, the Army never does what they schedule. So just get with Shelton's staff and write down a bunch of dates and they will never happen. Any dates they actually can do, and you can't, my unit will fill in with the 30 Fighter Squadrons we have access to." We got back to Pope AFB and I went back to my office thinking Duckworth will do like I recommended. Well, the next Thursday morning, I received a call from Colonel Nelson and he said "Hey Opie can you run over to Captain Duckworth's office and see what is going on. He hasn't called or come over here yet and we need this done tomorrow." I went over to Duckworth's office, which was down the street from my office, and I asked the office secretary where Captain Duckworth was. She said "Oh, he went on vacation last Friday." Just as she was saying this, Colonel Van Valkenburg (Duckworth's boss and my old squadron commander at Homestead) comes into the office area and said "Hey Opie, I believe that meeting last Friday didn't go very well and we can't do what General Shelton's staff wants. Can you go and smooth it all out for us. That is your job to work with the Army." I told him yes and went back to my office and called Colonel Nelson and when he answered I said "Colonel Nelson, the AF guys here said they don't want work with you." Nelson said "WHAT!" I said "Colonel Nelson, has my ALO/FAC unit ever let you down? Have we ever not gotten your troops the training they needed?" Nelson said "Yes Opie. You are right. Your unit has alway performed well." I said, "Sir, we will alway be there and we have 30+ fighter units available for training. The guys at Pope had no idea what they were trying to do and no business trying, but we will always be there and do our job." He agreed with me and said to have a great weekend. Several months later I was working directly with Colonel Nelson as we prepared to make a Combat Jump into Haiti and he never once questioned how we were going to support that operation. General Shelton made it clear to all AF and Army commanders that the ALO/FACs of my unit had his complete trust and not one bomb or bullet would be fired from an airplane (AC-130) or fighter jet or from a helicopter unless one of Opie's FACs is controlling the situation to prevent fratricide.

Within a year, that F-16 unit that Duckworth was in was disbanded and the jets sent to other bases.

Another difficult situation while I was an ALO/FAC happened soon after the events with Captain Duckworth and with the F-16 unit Duckworth flew with. Our unit had submitted a request to have Virginia Air National Guard F-16 support a local exercise with the Army. This request went to 9th Air Force Training at Shaw AFB, SC since they oversaw all fighter training on the east coast. Well a couple days later I received a call from Colonel Thompson at 9th AF Training asking if the Pope AFB F-16 unit (76th FS) could fill the mission because he had noticed that for the past year most of our fighter support had not been from 76th FS jets and that it would be cheaper to have them fly the missions versus farming out the training to aircraft out of state. I told Colonel Thompson "Sir, we have been asking the 76th FS to do the missions and they keep telling us that they don't do CAS mission (which really is one of their main jobs. They just didn't like doing it)." Colonel Thompson said "Opie, you go find that Squadron Commander and you tell him, HIS UNIT WILL START DOING CAS MISSIONS,

BEGINNING WITH THIS ONE. And if he says NO, then you call me from his office."

Now up to this point I had hoped and planned to fly F-16s again and stay at Pope AFB and be assigned to the 76th FS. So in a effort to look like a real combatant ALO/FAC, I put on face camouflage, my Kevlar helmet and checked out my M4 from the armory and headed to the 76th FS commanders office. Once there I knocked on his door and asked to come in. He said sure and waved me in. I said "Sir, we have a CAS mission coming up and 9th AF training wants your unit to fly the missions." He looked at me and chuckled and said "Come on, Captain Votipka, we already told you guys we don't do CAS, especially, night CAS (which was not true, they were flying the same F-16 Block 40 I flew at Homestead and had all the night IR equipment and targeting pods to do night CAS)." I thought to myself "Crap, what I am about to do by calling Colonel Thompson will end my chance to stay at Pope AFB and fly F-16s here". I looked at the 76th FS Commander and said "Sir, can I borrow your telephone?" He said "Sure, be my guest." I took the phone and dialed Colonel Thompson's office and he answered and I said "Colonel Thompson, I am at the 76th FS Commander's office and he said they will NOT support the CAS missions." Colonel Thompson said "Opie, please hand the phone to that commander." So I did and I could hear Colonel Thompson screaming from 10 feet way and that 76th FS Commander just stared at me and looked like he wanted to strangle me. And I'm just standing there thinking "I'm glad I brought my M4 and I guess I'm not going to fly F-16s at Pope now. I better start looking at other assignments." Finally, the 76th FS Commander hands me the phone and Colonel Thompson says "Opie, they will support that CAS mission and let me know if they ever say they won't support you guys in the future." I said thanks and hung up the phone and did an about face turn and walked out of the office.

Within a year, I was fully trained on the the F-15E heading to RAF Lakenheath. That 76th FS Commander ended up getting into trouble and was relieved of his command and the 76th FS closed its doors and the jets went to other bases.

What does Veterans Day mean to you?

Wonderful question.

I am thankful that Americans are willing to celebrate this day and recognize the millions of men and women who served our wonderful country. As opposed to Memorial Day, (which is a great idea to remember those who died for our country), Veterans Day was set up to celebrate everyone who served in peacetime and combat.

I think it is awesome that professional sports teams wear special uniforms in recognition of veterans because it puts that celebration in the hearts and minds of millions who might not think about the day.

Also, many restaurants and stores have Veterans Day sales and give discounts to veterans and it is a great show of appreciation.

Funny thing is, I have probably worked 30 of the 40 Veterans Days since I went in the military while banks and most government officials take the day off.

Do you have any interesting stories about aunts or uncles growing up?

My mother was the oldest of 10 children so I will go down the list by position in the family.

Uncle Ralph: As the oldest son he was named after Grandpa "RO" DeWald (Ralph Oscar). I was born on Uncle Ralph's birthday, 21 July, so my middle name is Ralph. Uncle Ralph served in WWII as a military policeman and remained in Germany with the Army for a few years after the war to help ensure safety and security of Germans. He married his wife Jeanie, who was German from Heidelberg, while he was stationed there. Ralph and Jeanie had 12 children. Ralph passed away of a heart attack at age 40. And Jeanie passed away recently.

Aunt Pat: She married Paul Hergott after WWII and had 16 children. Growing up, Aunt Pat was Grandpa DeWald's best cow milker (all by hand). She never really learned how to cook until she got married and didn't even know how to prepare hotdogs. She loved to play cards and alway made the best Rice Krispy treats. After raising 16 kids she opened a day care center and then worked at a nursing home until she was 85. She was older than most of residents she pushed around in wheel chairs. As the story goes, as a child she suffered from bad ear aches and infections. Then at about age ten, Grandpa DeWald had Grandma use a "home remedy" to cure her. Grandma collected a small cup of Pat's urine and then poured it in her ears. She never complained again about ear aches again (Pat didn't remember if the "home remedy" cured her or if she was too afraid to say she was in pain).

Uncle Ben: Uncle Ben married Bonnie and had 8 children. The only big thing I remember about Uncle Ben is that he had bought a new pickup truck and had no idea that it had a catalytic converter, nor knew what it did. They have been installed on all cars since the mid-1970s and they help burn up the unused fuel in automobile exhaust by heating up to several hundred degrees. Well, the first time he took this brand new truck to a wheat field and parked it in the middle of the wheat stubble (highly flammable straw). He parked the truck and got in his combine and went about cutting the rest of the wheat. After about 10 minutes, he looked across the wheat field and the whole area around his truck had caught fire from the super hot catalytic converter on the bottom of the truck and the fire burned up his new truck.

Uncle Phillip: Uncle Phillip married Dixie and had 7 children. Phillip served in Korea as a US Marine and he was a very tough man. When he was teenager he was in an alfalfa field baling hay and the baler seemed to be messed up. So instead of shutting the tractor and baler down, he decided to try to fix it by sticking his hand into the machine. The baler grabbed his hand and arm and tried to suck him in. But because he was very strong he was able to keep himself from getting sucked in for several minutes until his brother David noticed something was wrong from across the field and ran to help and shut the tractor down.

Uncle David: Uncle David married Doris (not his sister Doris) and they had 4 kids. The only real big thing I remember about him was his wisdom in telling truths. One time when he was 70, he told me that he couldn't believe the former Nebraska football coach, Tom Osborne, was thinking about running for NE Governor. Uncle David said "He's my age and I haven't had a new thought in 10 years. How does he think he is going to help make Nebraska better when he probably can't think of new stuff to do either?"

Aunt Doris: Aunt Doris married Les Henkel and they had 5 kids. She did and still loves to play cards and drink hot water (not hot tea or coffee). She and Les owned and ran the Tobias grocery store (the only grocery store my mom shopped at, and went once a month). When a fire destroyed their store, they became professional square dance callers and dancers and toured the country for hundreds of parties and contests.

Twins: Uncle Jean and Aunt Jane. Uncle Jean married Barbara and they had 3 children and Aunt Jane married Herb Cords and they had 4 children. Uncle Jean moved to Northern Nebraska so I really never knew him. Aunt Jane lived in Lincoln and would come down and play cards or when we took someone to the Lincoln airport we would stop and see her. Herb was in charge of all Lincoln Parks and Recreation department.

Uncle Mark: Uncle Mark joined the newly minted Peace Corps when he graduated from college (first of the family to do so I believe). President John F. Kennedy had just started the program and since President Kennedy was Catholic, the Peace Corps must have been a great idea. Uncle Mark served in Brazil for 2 years and really enjoyed it and was planning to stay there but Grandpa DeWald told him he had to come home and take over his farming from him, so he did. Uncle Mark was also in a serious car accident about 1/2 a mile from our house which killed our neighbor, Mr Stasnee, and permanently crippled Uncle Mark. He loved to play cards also and would come to our house and Grandma's and play cards.

What was Rhonda like?

Rhonda is probably the smartest of all us brothers and sisters.

She breezed through college and her master's degree and excelled in the research she did and became an outstanding dietician who loves and cares for so many hospitals and children's and mother's nutrition programs.

She was there for Mom after Daddy passed away and always helped cook and clean the house as we were growing up. School work seemed to come easy for her and she always had lots of friends.

She is amazing at baking, cooking, quilting and sewing. She makes a mean pot of chili and cinnamon rolls and can make runzas and brownies just like mom.

She is a long time volunteer fireman and EMT in Alexandria and helped keep that group of volunteers trained, fed, and made sure they had fun doing so.

She is very opinionated and is alway pretty sure she is right (and most of the time she is). She is very conservative in her values and loves her husband and their many pets with her whole heart and soul.

She has a very deep faith in God and serves her church and priest and fellow parishioners with the greatest love and kindness and is a gifted speaker during the Mass.

What was Mark like?

Mark probably has best leadership qualities in the family (John was probably a close second). Turner reminds me a lot of Mark in many ways.

Mark was an awesome mechanic and could fix and drive anything you gave him.

Mark has always had fun in everything he did and can get those around him to take part, do their best and have a blast while they do it.

Mark loves being around people and helping them be the best they can. He also is very dedicated to his friends and coworkers.

Mark is very conservative and loves his wife and daughter very much. He has a strong belief in God and serves his church and community.

Mark was and is very athletic and very, very, very, very competitive. He hates to lose and never gives up.

Mark is the best ping-pong player of my brothers and sisters and is on par with Andrew and Turner.

Mark loves the Nebraska Cornhuskers and is a diehard fan.

What was your brother John like?

F irst off, I want to remind everyone that John was 17 years old when I was born and joined the Army after he graduated from high school the next year before I was one so growing up I really didn't know him well but heard lots of stories about him growing up.

John was just over 6 feet tall so he towered over everyone in pictures you might see as he was growing up. He was the oldest of Grandpa and Grandma DeWald's 80 grandchildren so he was pretty much my mom and Grandma DeWald's favorite.

Growing up I was told that John was the typical FIRST born child - very obedient and tried hard to please his parents. He was very athletic and played football and basketball on his high school 8-man team. He only had 10 people in his class so everyone had to play to have a team. I remember him telling me that when his football and basketball teams would play Milligan HS his older cousin, on my dad's side, Raymond Turek would always play opposite him just to try to knock him down whether John had the ball or not.

John was a jokester and in HS enjoyed playing the Saxophone and even played in a 50's style music band for dances and parties and made some good coin doing it. When I would see him in Maryland he would say funny things like "we are having as much fun as real people" or "that dude is 5 feet tall and looks down on everyone."

John did well enough in school to be able to go to college, but in 1964 less than 20 percent of HS graduates went onto a 4 year college (no fluff degrees back then). You only went to "college" if you were going to be a doctor, lawyer, engineer, CPA, teacher, or RN, and there were no loan programs so you either joined the military to get the GI bill, got an athletic scholarship, or your parents paid the whole bill. Plus back then you didn't need a degree to get a good job and you could advance to the highest levels if you had a good work ethic. John proved it was possible. He told me that when he was in charge of the secret underground facility at Ft. Ritchie, PA with hundreds people designing and building computers for the government, many of the engineers that worked directly for him had Masters and PHDs from MIT or other prestigious engineering schools. Routinely, someone would come to his office and ask "John, why don't you hang up your diplomas from your Masters and PHD?" John would say "I don't have any, I didn't go to college." John would tell me that none of them believed him because they couldn't believe that they could be working for someone at such a high level that didn't have more eduction than they did. He also said that before some of their meetings started many of them bragged about graduating in the top 20 of their HS classes of several hundred. Some would say to John: "John, you must have graduated high in your HS class." John would look at them and say "Oh yes, I was number 10 in my graduating HS class." Then someone would say "Wow, that makes sense you did so well (thinking he had a class of 400-600 classmates)" and John would then say "Yes, I was number 10 of 10 students in my graduating class." He said no one ever believed him.

As I said, back in 1964, your parents had to pay for you to go to college. John told me that he thought about going straight into college but realized that if our parents paid college for him, they would be on the hook for 12 other kids and being the parent pleaser he was, he didn't want to set that standard. Also, as I said before, he knew a college degree wasn't a requirement to move up within a company in 1964. So he enlisted in the Army as a radio and TV repairman and was stationed in Seoul, Korea in late 1964 at the Army's Armed Forces Korean Network (AFKN) where he fixed their electronic equipment. Since there was an open spot for a radio DJ during the midnight to 4 AM time slot, he filled that position and 15 years later when my sister JoAnne was in the Army, a much older senior Sergeant saw her name tag and asked her if she was any relation to a Votipka who was an AFKN DJ in 1965. The Votipka name was distinct enough people recognized it many years later.

Back in 1964, US troops took a military troop ship to and from Korea and it stopped in Hawaii on the way. Grandma DeWald's young brother Edgar was a Navy Admiral (2 Star General) and was second in command of the US Pacific Fleet and stationed in Hawaii. Grandma DeWald sent Edgar a telegram stating that Little Johnny would be passing through Hawaii and she expected Edgar to take good care of her oldest grandson. John knew nothing about Grandma's telegram to Uncle Edgar and was just a new Army Private E-1 (lowest rank) as his boat steamed to Hawaii. As it approached the harbor, the troop ship's Captain was informed to have Private Votipka on the deck when they docked. The Captain, not knowing that Uncle Edgar was Little Johnny's great uncle, thought that Private Votipka was in trouble and was going to get hauled off to the Brig (military jail), so he had Private Votipka called up to the deck and was fussing him up and down for 15 minutes as the boat was readied for boarding. As Admiral Cruise's motorcade approach with police motorcycle escort lights flashing and sirens blaring, the ship's Captain again told lowly Private Votipka that he must really be in trouble that a whole motorcade was coming to get him. As Admiral Cruise boarded the troop ship, he didn't even salute the Captain but walked straight up to Private Votipka and grabbed him in a big bear hug and said "Little Johnny, how are you doing? Ferne told me to come get you and take good care of you and that's what I'm going to do." They left the boat and the Captain just stared with a flabbergasted look on his face. Little Johnny had a great 2 days touring Hawaii. Grandma was 5 feet tall and the matriarch of her 9 brothers and sisters. To her, Edgar was just her little brother who happened to be in the Navy, but Little Johnny was her oldest grandchild and Edgar had better take good care Little Johnny or suffer Grandma fussing him out.

While John was in Korea as a TV/Radio repairman in the spring of 1965, he and six other of his coworker (Army Privates and Sergeants) were sent to a little country most Americans never heard of "Vietnam" to set up an FM Radio retransmitting site that would allow American military advisers to have radio communications while in the valleys. His group spent a month building the retransmitting site on a mountain top. When done, they drew straws to determine which five soldiers were to stay and run the site for the next few months. John pulled one of the two long straws and got to return to Korea to finish his assignment and go back to the US. A month after he left Vietnam, he heard news that the North Vietnamese enemy (VietCong) destroyed the retransmitting sight and killed all five of the soldiers that were left there to keep it running.

John was a very practical person and got me on the track to look at cars as a mode of transportation and not something to spend a lot of money on if you could get a cheaper one that can do the same job. He was driving Hondas for 300,000 miles before most people trusted Hondas. He also traded electronic repair needed by an auto mechanic shop for free work done on his cars.

How did you meet your wife?

I love to tell this story because it shows how God works in our lives to get us to where he wants us to be.

I arrived from my tour in Korea in early January 1986, got checked out in my new unit, Bravo Company 1/82nd Attack Helicopter Battalion, and started to fly missions for the 82nd Airborne Division at Ft Bragg, NC. I also immediately started taking night and weekend college courses at the Embry-Riddle Aeronautical University International Campus on Ft Bragg in an effort to get my Bachelors Degree so I could become an Air Force or Navy Fighter pilot when I finished up my commitment to the Army in September of 1988. I was taking classes every week 4-5 nights a week and our semesters were actually 8 weeks long. In June of 1986 my company commander, Captain Greg Williamitis, asked me if I was interested in attending 3 weeks of parachute training in Ft Benning, GA since I was in the 82nd Airborne. It was something they wanted all officers and enlisted men to do. So I said yes and he got me a slot for the last week of August-second week of September. Since this was right in the middle of one of the 8 week Embry-Riddle semesters I was not able to take college classes 1 Aug - 30 September.

During the morning of Friday 1 August, 1986, I was at Simmons Army Airfield located on northern Ft Bragg and we planned and briefed a 4 aircraft mission would we be flying the next morning Saturday 2 August. At about noon because we would be working Saturday, Captain Williamitis told us to take the rest of the day off and be ready to fly the next morning. As I was driving my Yamaha 750 Maxim motorcycle out of the airfield I was thinking that since I didn't have any college classes to study for what was I going to do the rest of the day. At the stoplight right off the airfield I made the decision to make a left turn onto the road that would run into HWY 24 that would take me all the way out to Cherry Point Marine Corps Air Station where my cousin Joe DeWald was a C-130 Avionics Repairman. Three hours later I'm at his hangar and find out he is on vacation out of state. So three of his Marine friends invite me to go eat supper at the new Golden Corral or Ryans in Havelock when they get off work in 30 minutes. We ate supper and I told them I needed to head back because I had to fly in the morning. They said that they were going to a place called Chevys on Atlantic Beach and since it was on my way home that I should join them. So I did and about ten minutes after we get there one of them says to me "Ben, two really good looking women just walked in and you need to go talk to them." Well, I noticed one was a beautiful red head and I walked up to her and said something stupid because I was nervous and walked off. A couple minutes later I came back and introduced myself and tried to impress her by saying that I was a Cobra pilot (shockingly she knew what a Cobra Attack helicopter was) and we talked for about ten minutes. I told her I needed to head back to Fayetteville since I had to fly in the morning and I asked her if I could get her phone number. Only by God's grace she gave her phone number to me (and has probably regretted it for the last 36.5 years–haha). Two days later (Sunday afternoon) I found the phone number and figured that if it wasn't really her number it was probably to a Domino's pizza and I could order supper.

Well, after a few rings this really nice voice comes on the phone line.........

Just over a month later we were engaged and married 6 months later. If I didn't understand that God's timing is perfect, I would just write it off as we were just two meteorites crossing in the sky and accidentally crashed into each other. But the event that took place a year before in Korea, stopping me from extending my tour by six months, and then the event 9.5 years later of miraculously meeting the Chief Warrant Officer who denied my extension at the Ft Bragg Central Issue Facility showed me that God's plans are perfect in timing and that He is the true God who sees past, present, and future. God used this Chief Warrant Officer to stop me from extending in Korea so that a year later I would meet the LOVE of my life and then 9.5 years later allow me to meet this Chief Warrant Officer to bring closer for him. Almost ten years had past since he denied my extension and he remembered my name, where I was stationed, what I was flying, and that I was going to Ft Bragg. Out of 15,000+ pilots he had dealt with, having never met me face to face before, he recognized my last name and told me he was sorry for denying my extension and that they never denied an extension before me, nor did he deny an extension after me. When I shook his hand and told him that had he not denied my extension I probably would not be married to my beautiful wife and not have the wonderful three red headed sons I have. The look of relief on his face and smile showed me God set that meeting up 9.5 years prior so I could bring closure to his dread of denying my extension and showed me what an AWESOME, OMNISCIENT GOD I SERVE.

What's your favorite plane and why?

I love this question because it is easy. But before I start I would like to instead of the word "plane" I will use "aircraft because when most people hear "plane" they think of "airplane" and not "helicopter." I will also split this question into two different categories: My Favorite Aircraft (whether I personally flew it or not) and my favorite aircraft that I flew.

So let me start.

My favorite "aircraft" is the P-51 Mustang that was made famous during WWII and played a major role in the air war over Europe. It's my favorite because it is very cool looking and was a game changer in helping defend the US military Bombers flying to targets in Germany from England. The P-51 was the first aircraft that could escort the bombers all the way to their targets and back, preventing German fighter aircraft from shooting down large numbers of bombers heading to the targets.

The P-51 was designed to be easy to fly, fast, very maneuverable, heavily armed, and could fly very long distance and duke it up successfully with any enemy aircraft. Most WWII fighter planes were not easy to fly in aerial combat and the average ACE (at least 5 enemy aircraft kills) in most WWII fighters had over 500 hours (6-7 months) of flight experience in them before becoming an ACE. Due to the P-51's design, ACEs in the P-51 ranged from 7 hours of experience (first combat mission) to 700 hours experience. The P-51 itself was so good its capabilities could make an average novice pilot very good and out perform very experienced German pilots. I equate the P-51 Mustang to the modern day F-16: high performance single engine, single seat fighter that is easy to fly and allows average pilots to fly beyond their experience level.

P-51s

So now I will move onto my favorite Aircraft that I flew.

This is an easy one for me. My favorite aircraft that I flew was the AH-1F Cobra Attack Helicopter. Why did I like flying it and like the Cobra in general? It was a sleek looking, fast aircraft that was fun to fly and the tank killing mission and forward scouting mission were precarious and exciting. It was relatively easy to fly even though it was underpowered because it was a single turbine engine aircraft and because of all the weapons and electronic weapon systems that were put on it to do the mission. But it was very maneuverable and hard for the enemy to see because it was so narrow. It had the first helmet mounted sighting system that is commonplace today in modern attack helicopters and fighter jets. It performed many rolls and was the leading edge of an Army division's combat forces. It was such a good aircraft design that the US Marines still fly it today. They put new much lighter electronics in it, 2 larger turbine engines and a new stronger transmission. The thrill of the Single Engine one I flew was that you knew you had to be ready all the time for that lone engine to fail and since we alway flew "IN" or just on top of the trees and a lot of times at night there wasn't much margin for error. It was fun flying fast and low and protecting the Troop carrier helicopters like the UH-60 Blackhawk or CH-47 Chinhooks or UH-1H Hueys and the troops on the ground.

It didn't hurt that I just look very cool sitting in it. HAHA

What's cooler, flying helicopters, or jets?

This is probably the toughest question to answer.

I will answer it in two ways. First I will tell you what I believe (inside looking out) is cooler and why. Then secondly, I'll talk from what I believe (outside looking in) what most people think is cooler and why.

1. Having flown a wide variety of aircraft, both rotary and fixed wing, I personally believe flying helicopters are way cooler than flying jets. One reason I believe this is that a helicopter you have to "make" it fly. A helicopter running at full (100% power) will just sit there until the pilot manipulates the 3 sets of controls (collective, cyclic stick, anti-torque pedals) and forces or tells the helicopter what to do. And all this must be balanced correctly or the helicopter will spin out of control and crash. I relate it to someone who plays a drum set. A child can pick up sticks and thump the drums and hit the pedals for the bass drum and cymbals but it is loud and noisy and makes no sense. But a good drummer can manipulate the drum sticks on a wide variety of drums in the set and the use the foot pedals to make the bass drum beat and the cymbals clash and cause a crowd to get up and dance to music that is not only enjoyable but is fun to hear and sing and clap to.

As for the helicopter, this manipulation of the different controls must happen continuously from lifting off the ground into a stabilized hover, then into forward and skyward flight, then back to a hover and gently landing the helicopter back onto small place on the ground. All this while fighting the wind and turbulence and other forces of nature and all has to be done without thinking about every single movement that needs to be made to control the helicopter. It has to be like catching a baseball, you don't think about it. You just move your hand to the right spot in space and catch the baseball in midair.

Flying a helicopter is cool because you can truly hover on the side of a mountain just inches from the rotor blades hitting the rocks and pick up an injured person who fell off a cliff. Flying a helicopter in a small confined space of trees in an effort to hide from the enemy is cool because of the effort it takes to do that and not crash. Just lifting off the ground into a steady 5 foot hover and staying there while your fiancé is watching is just plain cool.

All fixed wing aircraft whether propeller to jets are designed to fly with little assistance. If a pilot trims the aircraft for takeoff and pushes the throttle to 100% power, unlike a helicopter that will just sit there, a fixed wing jet will accelerate and when it gets enough speed it will lift off the ground and climb until it runs out of fuel and require very little effort from the pilot (I will admit that landing a plane is not that easy). Flying a jet is fun, but it is normally hours of sheer boredom (cruise flight) interrupted by moments of sheer terror (diving at the ground to strafe or drop a bomb, or just trying to land it in bad weather).

Bottom line: I believe flying helicopters is cooler than jets because you have to MAKE a helicopter fly. A jet is designed (and will) fly on its own. And most of all hovering is just plain cool in and of itself.

2. Why do I think most people think it is cooler flying jets? I believe it it because jets are sleeker looking and faster and louder and they see them everywhere. Most people don't know how easy it is to fly a jet because that is what jets were designed to do and most movies glorify jet pilots over helicopter pilots. Most movies with jets have better actors (Top Gun) versus helicopters (Firebirds).

Bottom line: Had I not flown helicopters I would still believe jets are cooler but since I have experienced both I can truly say that FLYING HELICOPTERS IS WAY COOLER THAN JETS.

If I could make as much money flying helicopters as I do flying jets I would be flying a helicopter tomorrow. But since most helicopters only carry a few people at a time versus 175 paying passengers, helicopter jobs will never pay as well. Since I DIDN'T say flying jets wasn't cool at all (I just said not AS cool as a helicopter) I will continue to do a job that is a little LESS COOL but pays better. I will get my COOL fix from flying the little Green Aeronca Champ out of a grass runway in Red Oak. The Aeronca Champ and the Piper Cub were the helicopters of the pre-helicopter flying days. They can almost hover and can land about anywhere, so for now they are as close to flying a helicopter I can get.

Tell us a good Hal Hughes story

First of all I want to let everyone know some information about who Hal Hughes is and how I got to know him.

Most people only know Hal is an old Army buddy and an insurance agent who has help me prepare myself and my family for events we hope never happen.

Hal is 16 years older than me and he served in the Air Force as an Avionics/Electronics technician and severed in Vietnam in the Mid-1960s. Hal was in the Air Force over 12 years and then got out, completed his degree and became an Insurance agent in the 1970s. In 1979 Hal decided he wanted fulfill his dream of being a pilot but was too old to go to Air Force Pilot training, so he decided to enlist in the Army as an Infantryman because he knew he could get promoted faster in the Infantry and have a better shot of getting selected for Army Warrant Officer pilot training (WOFT). The Army didn't have an age limit if you were in the Army. So at age 32, Hal went through Army Infantry Basic Training and Infantry training. He got stationed at Ft Lewis, WA where I would be stationed as a UH-60 helicopter mechanic.

In October 1983, I was selected to attend WOFT. Nine other Ft Lewis soldiers were also selected but 3 were unable to attend it on such short notice. So Hal was called and asked if he could attend the short notice class and he said yes. We both arrived at Ft Rucker, AL ten days later and we were put in the same class 84-11. On November 1, we started class and Hal and I agreed to be paired together to help each other in the barracks and academics. Hal was now 36 and I was 20. Hal was great at shining boots and I was good at cleaning and setting up our mandatory displays and washing clothes. So Hal made sure our boots were shiny and I cleaned and pressed our uniforms. This initial phase was just academics and Officer training and was called WOC-D (Warrant Officer Candidate Development).

On January 3rd, we moved onto the next phase which was Primary Flight training where we were to learn how to fly the TH-55. During this 3 months of training we had to continue to live in barracks and had to have all our uniforms and equipment ready for inspection all while learning how to fly a helicopter. At the end of this 3 months, as part of our Officer training we had to have our rooms and uniforms ready for a final inspection. Hal and I were roommates and were prepared to for this inspection (or we thought we were).

So here is the first GOOD Hal story:

During our training in WOC-D we spent one day at an obstacle course called Leadership Reaction Course (LRC). At the end of the day, we were waiting for the bus to get us and we were waiting near a base swimming pool. We had 2 assigned instructors and one was brand new at the job. Well...... Hal had heard a rumor that at the LRC it was the responsibility of the WOFT cadets to throw the the new Instructor in the swimming pool. So for most of the day during LRC Hal was telling everyone that we had to do this and that at the end of the day he would give the signal and we would call pick up the new Instructor and throw him in the cold water in the pool.

All of us were thinking that would be a stupid idea but didn't tell Hal how we felt, figuring he wouldn't have the guts to do this. Well lo and behold at the end of the day as we stood around the swimming pool with very cold water, Hal screamed out loud "Let's get him." Hal ran straight for the new Instructor (expecting all of us to join in), picked him up in a bear hug and leaped into the cold water while carrying the Instructor. This completely caught the instructors off guard, especially the new instructor. As Hal and this new instructor came up out of the water, the new instructor looked as if he was going to kill Hal with his bare hands. The older instructor was laughing uncontrollably. We all stood there in disbelief that Hal actually did this and we all thought Hal was going to booted from the program. The new instructor started to yell at Hal and had him doing pushups until we got on the bus. Needless to say, Hal didn't get kicked out.

Here is a second story about Hal:

During our final inspection of Primary flight training Hal and I were roommates and the Instructors found 3 things wrong with our uniforms and our displays so we failed the inspection. So they moved us into different rooms, not together, and after a week we were to be inspected. Hal didn't clean out all the drawers in his new room because he thought the previous person probably had cleaned everything. So during the next inspection, I passed with no issues, but when they inspected Hal's room they found 3 dead cockroaches in the drawers Hal didn't clean so he failed a second time and was put up for elimination from the WOFT program. During his elimination interview with the Brigade command, the commander found out Hal had served in Vietnam like he had and was an avid turkey hunter like he was. So the commander decided to give Hal another chance and leave him in the program. One good thing about this last process was that Hal ended up washing back 2 classes instead of 1 class. Had he just been set back 2 weeks versus 4 weeks, there is a very good chance Hal would have been paired up with the training students that were killed in helicopter cash one month later. God was humbling him and watching out over him.

What was your first boss like?

Wow that is a tough question because it depends what you call a "Boss."

If you mean by "Boss" someone who pays you a salary or that supervises you I have an answer for that question. If you mean by "Boss" someone who tells you what to do or sets your schedule then that would be my Dad and older brothers. But I don't think that is what you are asking.

So my "What was your first boss like" answer will be written for different phases of my life and they will have been people who were supervisors at a paying job or bosses that actually paid my salary.

My first "Boss" at a paying job was while I was in high school. I had a job running the projectors at the Hebron movie theater and setting up the billboard out front of the theater. My "Boss was a middle-aged woman who I basically never saw. She would leave me letters of instruction on the candy concession stand because I would show up for work at 6pm on Saturdays (movies only played on Fridays and Saturdays) and unlock the building and set up the movies on the projectors. At the end of night after I cleaned up I would change the billboard to display the next weekend's movie and lock up. So I can say my boss was great because I almost never saw her and she trusted me to get everything done. She really showed my as a boss what my Grandpa DeWald used to say: "People won't be trustworthy if you don't trust them." Or she might have thought I smelled bad and didn't want to be around me. I never asked so I will never know. Haha.

The summer between my junior and senior year in high school I worked part time for a farmer that lived a few miles from our farm. He was a very busy farmer and his kids had graduated and left home and needed help spraying his corn for weeds and moving irrigation pipe. He also was very trusting and basically would tell me what needed to be done that day and left me to do it. So again I had a boss that didn't hover over me and trusted me to get everything done. Since I got it done he never had to deal with me much other than tell me what he needed completed.

When I went to Army Basic training my first boss was Sgt First

Class (E-7) Brunson. SFC Brunson had served in Vietnam as an Infantryman and now was my Drill Sergeant. SFC Brunson was a 6' 3" black man who bragged that his arms were so long that he could scratch his knees without bending over. He would often say he could punch you without moving even if you were 6 feet away. So what was he like as a boss? He was tough and didn't take any guff from anyone. He was very experienced as an instructor and a very good shot with the M-16 and because of his size he was very intimidating.

I would like to finish by saying I was very privileged to have many "bosses" my whole life who trusted me and allowed me to not have to have an 8-4 work schedule which allowed me to set my own schedule to a large degree.

Are you still friends with any of your friends from high school? How have they changed since then?

There are two main guys I have continued to remain in contact with on a pretty continuous basis. Since I went to school with many of my cousins, I have continued to see them at least every couple years.

The main friend I have continued to remain in contact with is Greg Bodtke. He visited me a couple times when I was in the Army and I visited him every time I went to Nebraska. Greg was also in my wedding as a groomsman and I was a groomsman in his wedding.

How has Greg changed? To be honest, Greg is still the same nice, easy going person he was back in high school. Greg still sings in several church and local choirs and plays the trombone in at least 2 or 3 music groups. Like me, Greg has some gray hair and looks a little older but overall hasn't changed much.

The other person is Jeff Retzlaff. He is my brother-in-law's nephew and lived with us several years while growing up. How has Jeff changed? Like Greg, Jeff hasn't changed much. Over the years he has worked many different jobs and has learned how to do everything from building a house from the ground up to totally rebuilding a vehicle from junk to a fully functioning automobile.

Overall, their personalities haven't changed. They are still the wonderful life enjoying men who are family men and hard working men.

What was your Mom like when you were a child?

My mother loved to play cards and dominos (not the pizza).

She loved to garden and teach first and second graders Catechism at church for most of her adult life. My mother enjoyed doing family events with her parents, brothers and sisters. She was always happy to have big family get togethers and cookouts.

Mom loved God and loved to attend daily mass and recited the Rosary daily. She loved to serve her church and her priest by doing things like laundry and cleaning the pews and building. Mom loved to sing the hymns and because of her high, squeaky voice you could her her from anywhere in the church.

Mom loved children and was extremely pro-life and very patriotic and served in many positions within community groups to make the local community better.

Mom loved to travel by car, train, and airplane to go see family. At the airport she loved to "people watch" as she called it. She loved people and enjoyed just imagining what their lives were like based on the looks on their faces and the way they dressed.

What were your favorite toys as a child?

I had a few favorite toys. One was the original Tank verses Tank video game. It was a very rudimentary game like Pong. Another was our ping pong table and the many games we have played there.

We made many of our own toys. We made bows and arrows and swords and shields that we used to play cowboys and Indians. We also crossbows that we could shoot homemade arrows on that went much further than our bows could. We also made sling shots and the rock throwing sling like David in the Bible used to take down Goliath.

We had a sand pit in our side yard and like any kids we played with toys and little trucks and tractors.

How has your life turned out differently than you imagined it would?

As a young kid I thought I would be a super hero like Shazam or the Flash. That didn't happen, Haha.

While in high school I imagined I would go to the Army and learn how to fix and fly helicopters and after five or six years, move back from Nebraska and become a crop duster like a former Vietnam pilot in Hebron named Wayne Henning.

I did imagine I would marry a beautiful woman I would met while in the Army and have several children but I never thought about living in the state of the wife I would marry some day.

I never had any intention of making a career out of the military, but after every school/training I went to I owed more time to the military. The initial Army commitment was three years, Army pilot training commitment was four years, Air Force pilot training was eight years, and moving to new bases was two years, and my pilot bonus was a five year commitment. Now most of the moves to new bases was concurrent with the longer commitments I owed so most of the time it didn't matter about getting a new commitment for moving or training. But I ended up doing 20 years, 4 months and 8 days on active duty because my pilot bonus took me to February 15 of 2003 (just short of 20 years and 4 months). Your retirement date has to be at the end of the month.

Basically, there was a price I paid to go to the many schools I went to and the places we got to live and that price was owing more time to the military.

I did think that while in the military I would go back to Nebraska more often than we did to see family and do some farm work and show my children how to drive a tractor and haul bales and hunt. But I had no idea that raising a family used up most of your extra money and that plane tickets for 5 were expensive and that driving would use up a lot of the little free time we would have to travel.

While in the military I had no intention of becoming an airline pilot because I never met one and I thought it would be a very boring job. I really didn't know how much time away from home an airline pilot spent, nor how much money they were paid. All I wanted to do was defend our country against the Commies and have fun flying and doing other military stuff.

When I had 15 years in the military, my plan for after completing my 20 year career was to move back to North Carolina and become a school teacher and be home every night. But when we moved to Columbus AFB, MS (prior to 9/11) pretty much all the other pilots were talking about becoming airline pilots. God had me meet a senior SWA Captain, Mark Jensen, who had flown F-4s in Vietnam and he explained all the good and bad of being an airline pilot and informed me that Baltimore would be a big domicile for SWA.

I knew I wanted to have kids but had no idea what all that entailed. I knew it would be fun and that being a Dad and Granddad would be a gift from God. But I truly didn't have much of an idea or forethought what that would all look like.

Bottom Line: Yes my life has on one hand turned out differently than I imagined as a farm boy from Nebraska. But I know now that God's plans are much bigger and better than an immature teenager could ever imagine and that has been my best surprise as I have gotten older seeing God's hand in everything I have done (even when I made a too quick decision to do something.) God has blessed me with a beautiful wife, three godly sons who have grown to be awesome husbands and dads, a daughter I'll get to meet again and hug when I get to Heaven, and a van load of AWESOME GRANDKIDS that remind me daily of God's love and grace. If my life was a movie, I could not have written a better script than God has written. In many, ways my life had turned out like I had dreamed in my youth, but over all it has turned out to be so much better. I praise Jesus Christ, my Lord and Savior for all that He has done in my life and for using me in the the many ways He has throughout my life.

GOD IS GOOD!!!!!!

Did you ever get in trouble at school as a child?

THIS QUESTION IS EASY TO ANSWER: WELL YES I DID, and there aren't enough pages in write about it all. Hahaha I really only remember a couple of times I got in trouble in K-12 schools. Once when I was in the fourth grade I talked too much and interrupted the teacher and I was not allowed to play outside at the lunchtime recess. I had to remain in the classroom and write "I will not talk in class" one hundred times on the chalk board.

When I was in the fifth grade, our whole class got in trouble for being too loud and all 32 of us had to stay after school and get a lecture from the principal. The really bad part of this was that I lived 12 miles away and my parents policy was that if we got in trouble at school and missed the bus because we had to remain after school was out, my parents would not come and get us. We had to walk home. Luckily for me, my principal grew up with my oldest brother and he felt bad for me. He ended up driving me and another student who lived on the way to my house.

Other than those two incidents I don't really remember getting into too much other trouble because I feared having to walk home if I had to stay after school.

Was there anything unusual about your birth?

As far as I know, there was nothing unusual in my area of Nebraska about being born number 12 and having a mother that was 39 years old at the time. Many families were large at the time and not unusual.

I wasn't a tiny baby, nor a large baby like some of my grandchildren. I was just average size and born in a hospital in Fairbury, Nebraska.

I did have pointy ears so I kind of looked like an elf, but I'm pretty sure I wasn't an elf. I just looked like one.

What gives you peace of mind?

Wonderful question.

The most important and biggest thing that gives me peace of mind is that I have accepted Jesus Christ as my Lord and Savior. I know that one day I will be in Heaven bowing down in His presence.

I also have peace of mind in the fact that I know God is completely in control of everything and therefor there is no reason to be worried.

Another thing that gives me peace of mind is the fact that I have a wonderful wife and family that love me and will always be there for me.

At work I have peace of mind because I have extensive experience and know that with God's help I can get through any situation.

What is one of the best shows you've ever been to?

I have a couple answers to this question because it depends on what you mean by "shows".

If you mean "plays" or "concerts", then I would have to say it is a tie between "West Side Story" and "Seven Brides for Seven Brothers" performed by Nash Central High School when Andrew and Daniel were part of the cast. The music and acting was really good and I enjoyed watching everyone work hard and enjoy themselves.

If you mean "Air Shows", then it would have to in 1974 when my Dad took several of us kids to the Lincoln, NE airshow. The USAF Thunderbirds performed flying the awesome F-4 Phantom II

(Double Ugly). They buzzed the crowd at 200 feet while flying 500 mph and were super loud and really put on a great demonstration of air power. The next year the Thunderbirds switched from the combat proven monster twin engine Fighter/Bomber to the tiny and less noisy USAF Advanced pilot training jet the T-38 Talon. The Navy also switched from the F-4 to the tiny little A-4.

I was thankful to have gotten to see the mighty F-4

before they made the switch to a jet so much smaller that it was actually hard to see when it would doing the demonstration.

The Mighty F-4 Phantom II

Air Force Thunderbird and Navy Blue Angel

A-4 used by the Blue Angels

What are your favorite songs?

"Lead Me" by Sanctus Real: A song all husbands and fathers need to know the lyrics to.

"God's Not Dead" by the Newsboys: A song we need to shout everyday from the roof tops and at the top of our lungs.

I really like the 'The Voice of Truth" and "Broken Together" by Casting Crowns: Both have gospel truths about serving God and loving each other as a husband and wife.

"Hungry like a Wolf" by Duran Duran "Jessie's Girl" and "Love Somebody" by Rick Springfield "What does the Fox Say" by Yivis: It's just a funny song "Cat's in the Cradle" by Harry Chapin. It's a sad tale of a dad who traveled too much and missed his son growing up but alway had the hope he would find time to do thing with his son. But as his son grew older the son had his own life and didn't have time for his father. As a self diagnosed Workaholic, I would listen to this song to remind myself that I needed to make time for my wife and children. Because in the end no-one ever wishes they had spent more time at work.

Have you ever sleep walked or sleep talked?

Personally, I have never noticed if I have "sleep walked and/or talked" because I was asleep. Haha

Now having said that, several family members, especially my wife have told me that I have, and I don't doubt them because it seems to align with the dream I was having at the time.

Luckily for me I never got hurt or hurt someone else while I was "sleep walking and/or talking."

At what times in your life were you the happiest and why?

My most happiest day was 28 Mar 1987 when I married my beautiful wife Pam because she was so beautiful and radiant on our wedding day.

When I meet Pam and when I asked her to marry me and she said yes were very happy times indeed because I knew then our lives would be wonderful together.

The birth of our three sons Daniel, Andrew, and Turner were extremely happy events because I knew they were a blessing from God.

The loss of our daughter Theodosia was a very sad day because I alway pictured myself raising a daughter and walking her down the aisle at her wedding.

My first solo flight in a TH-55 helicopter in Army pilot training was happy because I proved to myself I was capable of being a pilot.

My first solo flight in a T-37 jet in AF pilot training because it fulfilled my dream of flying jets.

Graduation from Army Pilot training and pinning on my Army Pilot wings was awesome because it was the start of a fun career.

Graduation from Air Force Pilot training and pinning on my Air Force Pilot wings was wonderful because I had for some reason thought it was impossible for someone like me.

How did you get to school as a child?

$\diamond$

This is simple. Every morning at 7:45 AM we rode the public school bus. When I went to Meridian school system (K-4) everyone not in after school activities rode the bus to Alexandria Elementary/Junior High (4-8 grades) in the morning and then those going to grades 1-3 got on a bus to Daykin and those going to 9-12th grade got on a bus to Tobias.

When we switched to Hebron school system, again if not in after school activities we road the bus at 7:50 to Hebron.

For after school activities we drove our own car to school.

What is one of the greatest physical challenges you have ever had to go through? What gave you strength?

Great question.

I believe one of the top physical challenges was US Army Basic Parachutist training at Ft Benning, GA. It was physically challenging because it was the last week in August 1987 and first two weeks in September 1987 (three of the hottest weeks of the year). We went "Black Flag" by 11am every morning meaning it was too hot and humid to do outside work for more than 30 minutes at a time. So, every thirty minutes they would stop our training and tell us to drink water and 10 minutes later start training again. Luckily training started at 5:30am so it wasn't as hot as the latter part of the day. What got me through it was the fact that I was in very good physical shape and I had been living in NC for 8 months and had climatized myself during the summer months. Plus, everyone was wearing the new Army BDUs (Battle Dress Uniform) which only came in winter weight (because we thought we would first WWIII in much cooler Europe). Since I was already stationed at Ft Bragg, NC, the 82nd Airborne Division was still issuing Vietnam War era light weight jungle fatigues. So I was much cooler than everyone else. ONLY problem was that I looked totally different than the 300 soldiers in my training unit. But I totally didn't care because I was much cooler during training.

Winter Weight BDUs

Vietnam War Jungle Fatigues

Army Basic Training was very challenging but I was in very good physical shape.

Army Warrant Officer Training was physically challenging also but again I was in excellent physical shape.

High School wrestling season every year was very physically challenging but our coach always got us in good shape.

If you had to go back in time and start a brand new career, what would it be?

$$\diamond$$

WOW, that is a great question.

When I was in High School, Computer Systems Analyst was an up and coming new thing. Basically it was someone who wrote code to run computer systems (hardware programming) and not the software programming like we have today. It seemed exciting and leading edge.

But knowing what I know today and if I had to start a different career 40+ years ago, I believe I would have become a tax account and CPA. Then, after getting some experience in tax preparation I would have attended law school and became a tax attorney and helped defend individuals, families, and companies from state and federal IRS overreach.

I believe I would have enjoyed that career path versus the computer systems path because the computer world has changed so rapidly and constantly over the past 40 years that it would have been tough to keep up with it all, whereas accounting and taxes haven't changed at such a fast rate. I would have felt like I was fighting for the underdog against the big government.

Tell me about a time you volunteered for something that nobody else wanted to do.

❦

I actually have two really good examples. No, technically I didn't initially volunteer for these things. Someone came to me in both situations because they knew I was stupid enough to say yes if asked.

When I was flying AH-1 Cobras at Ft Bragg in November of 1986 we were on a week long exercise flying out of McEntire Air National Guard base just east of Columbia, SC. About four days into the exercise, one of the Cobras had an electrical issue and landed in the middle of a field about 60 miles from McEntire. The mechanics went there and could not fix it there because they didn't have all the necessary tools. I would need to be taken back to McEntire where the proper tools could be used. The aircraft could start and they believed one radio worked but none of the lights worked and it was getting dark and we couldn't send a flatbed truck and trailer for several days. So someone would have to guard it until we could flat bed it out. Plus we would have to get a crane to pick it up and put it on the flat bed trailer.

My Commander, Captain Williamitis, came up to me and said "Ben, I need you to go with Sargent Tims and his crew to bring back that Cobra to McEntire tonight. Sargent Tims will be flying in the front seat with you because all the other pilots said they don't want to fly that aircraft at night. Any questions?" I said "None at all Sir. When does the vehicle leave to go to the Cobra?" An hour and half later, I was started the Cobra and took off. Roughly two hours after we left McEntire to get it, I was landing that Cobra back at McEntire and two days later it was fixed.

The second one was while I was the Chief of T-37 flight training at Columbus, AFB. One of the 150 T-37 instructor pilots came to my office and said "Opie, one of our student pilots needs to be sent on their solo flight tomorrow and we would like you to do it." I said "Why me, I've never flown with this student and why doesn't the student's assigned instructor or any of the other instructors do it?" He said "Well, this student has a great attitude, but we are all scared to solo the student out because we are afraid the student might crash. But if we don't solo the student out tomorrow we will have to wash the student out of flight school." I said "Ok, I will be there at 9am tomorrow morning."

The next morning I briefed the student on what we were going to do. Normally for a solo flight the instructor and student would fly together for thirty minutes and then they would land and the instructor would get out and the student would go fly three patterns solo. This day, we took off and after an hour of flying I knew the only issue was the student's confidence level was low and was afraid to go solo. We landed and pulled into parking. I got out of the T-37 and turned around and the student was starting to get out also. I asked "Where are you going?" The student said "Well aren't we done? I don't have enough fuel to go solo." I said "Get back in that seat, I am having the fuel truck fill up the tanks. You are going solo!" The student's eye got really big but got back in the seat. I got the fueling completed, signaled to start both engine and saluted the student and walk back to the Squadron building where I called the instructors that ran the miniature control tower for the T-37 runway and told them, "Hey this is Opie. Student [So-and-So] is taxiing for takeoff. You may have to tell the student to POINT the aircraft at the ground and land, and you may have to do that three times." They said they would. I got a radio and listened and the first pattern the student came around the aircraft went straight through and didn't land. The second pattern the student came around the instructor in the tower yelled over the radio "POINT YOUR AIRCRAFT AT THE GROUND" and the student did and did a good landing and took back off. This happened two more times and the student after doing the three required landings, taxied back to parking and got out with the biggest smile. The student's confidence was now high and ended up finishing the program and became a USAF pilot. Many of the instructors came to me after this and were in amazement that I was able to accomplish soloing the student and couldn't believe how I had the guts to do it. I told everyone of them "Look, I grew up flying when it was not uncommon for planes to crash and pilots to get killed. It was the cost of doing business. We had two crashes in my Army pilot Training class. I felt the student had a 50/50 chance of making the landings without crashing and that the student needed a confidence boost and soloing would be that boost. Plus the aircraft has an ejection seat, so there was always a back up plan."

What is the most memorable adventure you ever had with your wife/children?

WOW that is hard to narrow it down to a "most memorable" adventure. Pam and I had so many memorable trips moving to new assignments and each and everyone of those were wonderful adventures.

But I believe it would have to our family trip to Europe from England in the summer of 1997 when we were stationed at RAF Lakenheath, UK.

Why was it memorable?

Well for one thing it was the longest trip we took as a family together and my mother and her sisters, Pat, Doris, and Jane, came with us on this trip.

As a family we got to travel via boat from England to Cherbourg, France. Then we got to visit the D-Day Memorial and beaches.

The boys got to see Pam's great uncle's grave there at the Normandy Cemetery. We got to visit many places in France and then off to Italy to see the Leaning Tower of Pisa and then to Rome. I had the pleasure of see my sons get to interact and play cards with my aunts and mother.

We got a personal tour of the Vatican and toured the Vatican Art museum and the Sistine Chapel. We enjoyed seeing the Colosseum and finding out it was taken apart and the stones were used to build St. Peter's Cathedral.

From Rome we traveled to Klagenfurt, Austria to spend a few days with a DeWald relative, Professor Wolfgang Moracher and his family, touring the local area and castle. And then off to Salzburg Salt Mines for a fun tour of the underground mine. We got to travel through Switzerland and Germany. We visited the Neuschwanstein castle located in the village of Hohenschwangau, Allgau, Bavaria which Disney based its Sleeping Beauty castle after. The back through Luxembourg and the Ardennes Forest (think Battle of Bulge) and back to the ship to head back to England. It was a great trip.

I was blessed to have done a lot of traveling and sightseeing with Pam and the boys throughout the United States, England and Europe. It was all enjoyable and a wonderful experience.

What does it feel like flying in a jet? (Question from Bennie)

I have gotten this question a lot over the years and I will try to describe everything the best I can.

Just like there are different modes of transportation and different environments we travel in; I will try to use different examples to help you visualize what it is like to fly a jet. When I say jet, I mean a military fighter jet versus a commercial airliner which are technically high bypass turbo-fan aircraft. The original airliners were turbo-jet aircraft.

I will start out with describing what it was like flying a helicopter. Helicopters are very complex machines that require the pilot to constantly manipulate three sets of controls to sustain controlled powered flight: Cyclic stick (makes you go forward, backward, left, and right), collective stick (makes you go up and down and go faster in the direction you want to fly), anti-torque pedals (used to keep the nose of the aircraft pointed straight instead of turning in the opposite direction of the main rotor torque and they can make the aircraft turn left or right rotating around the center of the aircraft). It is like being a drummer playing a drum set with several different types of drums and cymbals trying to produce sounds that are meaningful to the song being played.

Flying a helicopter is the equivalent of riding in an old-fashioned horse drawn wagon over a bumpy dirt road with you in the back trying to play your drum set. It's loud and bumpy and constantly moving, vibrating, shaking and sometimes has a mind of its own for which you must constantly be counteracting. When you hear a helicopter pilot on the radio his/her voice sounds like the played one of the Munchkins in the Wizard of Oz. WaWe Arrrrr MmmMuncccchkins fffffrrummm MmmMuuuncccchhkinnn Lala Laaandd. But flying them is super fun because all the things they can do like, hover, fly backwards, climb straight up, and fly low level at the tops of the trees. You feel like you have accomplished something significant on each flight because you made it takeoff and fly and land. Airplanes will fly if you get them going fast enough (landing is hard) but helicopters need to be forced into the air by the pilot manipulating the controls.

Small private airplanes like the Aeronca Champ I am part owner of is like riding a lawnmower with wings. It is loud, shakes and vibrates a lot, sometimes dusty and doesn't go much faster than a car. They are fun to fly and try to land but doesn't require anywhere near the complex feet and hand coordination a helicopter does.

Just getting up in the air and seeing the sights and traveling to a destination is fun and challenging in its own way.

Commercial aircraft like the Boeing 737 like I currently fly are the equivalent of strapping large wings on a large passenger bus. It's not too noisy, nor is it too bumpy, but it is louder than being in a car and sometimes because of turbulence it can have some uncomfortable bumps. Boeing 737s, like buses, can go as fast as many vehicles one third their size. But because of their size and weight they have a lot of wind resistance and can't go as fast as small sports cars like Ferraris and Corvettes or military fighter jets. Commercial airliners like buses are not very maneuverable because of their size and weight. When you try to turn them, you put in the steering command then wait a second for it to start to turn. Then, as it begins to turn you have to make an opposite direction input to get it to stop turning and go the direction you want it to go. But one really nice thing about driving a bus or flying a commercial airliner is that unlike a small car or fighter jet, you can stand up and stretch your legs or have use of a bathroom.

Sooooo, what is it like to fly a jet (Fighter Jet for this story)?

Flying a military fighter jet is a lot like driving an ULTRA-High-Performance sports car like a Ferrari, Corvette, Lamborghini. ......

It has a very small, cramped cockpit or cabin area with a seat that fits you very tight, so you don't move around much when maneuvering quickly. The whole experience is like putting on a very nice pair of gloves, "comfortable but slightly restrictive." Like an expensive sports car, getting strapped into a fighter jet is actually like "strapping on" the jet. What I mean by this is that when strapping on a jet (or a sports car) you are actual make it part of you, making it an extension of your mind and body. You maneuver it and manipulate it just as you would your arm or leg or hands or fingers. Like expensive sports cars, fighter jets are very fast and nimble. They can accelerate extremely fast, stop quickly, and turn very sharply and quickly. From a standing start when you gun the engine to full power you are pushed back into your seat and when you are screaming along at very high speeds and then turn, you can feel the increased G-loading on your body as the jet/car does everything it can do to turn as tightly as physically possible.

A fighter jet, like a sports car, can travel at very high speeds and because the cockpit is so small, and you are traveling so fast the cockpit/cabin area is actually very quiet. Since the air conditioner doesn't have to cool a very large area, you never have an issue keeping cool, even on the hottest days.

As for speed, a sports car doing 200 mph will actual feel faster than being in a fighter jet going supersonic or 800 mph at 40,000' because the feeling of speed it relative to how close to the ground you are. This illusion is called "Motion Parallax," which states that the closer you are to something while you are moving, will feel like it's moving faster past you than something in the distance. A great illustration of this is: You are on the highway traveling at 70 mph parallel to a mountain range in the distance. As you pass by a farmer's picket fence at 70 mph the pickets in the fence become a blur but the mountain range in the distance don't seem to be moving at all. So, while driving a sports car on the ground moving over 100 mph will seem like your surroundings are flashing past you. In a fighter jet at 40,000' going 800 mph the ground and trees will seem like they are hardly moving, but in that same Jet at 100' the trees and ground will be zooming by at a tremendous speed.

Fighter jets fly as smooth as they look sleek from the outside and you can make them do almost any maneuver you can think of in your head and can do them rapidly and get to where you want to go very quickly.

How did I get to where I'm at today, flying Boeing 737s as a Captain for Southwest Airlines?

BENEDICT R. VOTIPKA, Southwest Airlines Captain, BWI. (As an imposter, I think to myself everyday: Catch me if you can Mr. Policeman)

Before I get started, I first want to thank my parents for wanting to have 13 children so I could be around for all my adventures and to God for protecting me and putting wise men and women in my path to mentor me.

What a beautiful morning it was as I took off for the short flight from ORF to BWI. I leveled off at 16,000ft just above the clouds, briefed the arrival, approach, and landing in BWI. Having a few minutes to enjoy the view, I looked out the left cockpit window of this Boeing 737-700 and glance back at the wing and awesome sensation of speed as we skirted the clouds at 300 knots. I thought to myself, "I've gotten away with it again." The descent, approach, and landing are uneventful. As I turn off runway 33L and maneuver into gate A5, the ground guide gives me the stop and chocked signals. I shutdown the engines and I immediately notice several police cars circle the aircraft and a fully kitted up SWAT team running up the jet bridge stairs. With nowhere to escape I get out of my seat and open the cockpit door. I am met with several M-4s pointing at me and a man, flashing his badge at me, says, "Benedict Votipka, you are under arrest for pretending to be a pilot, impersonating a military officer, and downright tomfoolery." I lower my head, extended my wrists to be handcuffed and say, "The gig is up, guilty as charged. I am an IMPOSTER."

Throughout the past 42+ years, I have either been told outright (or it has been implied) that I couldn't be a military pilot, let alone an airline pilot. So many people believe there is one cookie cutter way to becoming a captain at a major airline. One example is: first born son, A+ student, attend and graduate top of your class from the Air Force or Naval Academy with an Aeronautical Engineering degree, graduate top of pilot training class and go on to fly fighters. Too often I hear young people say that it would be cool to be a pilot/doctor/coach, but I can't because I don't fit the mold. I quickly tell them yes you can. There are 300 million people in America and there are 300 million ways to accomplish your dreams. I was told many years ago that the #1 reason people fail at accomplishing their dream is because they don't START. You will never make those millions from your invention you have in your head if you keep putting it off until tomorrow. Tomorrow never comes. When I mentor my kids and other young people, I tell them one thing I have learned is not to come up with 10 reasons why you CAN'T do something. Come up with 1 reason to do it that is legal and moral, and get at it. I tell them not to take NO for an answer and if someone says it can't be done, don't listen. People who say things can't be done are usually interrupted by people doing it.

How did I get to where I'm at today, flying Boeing 737s as a captain for Southwest Airlines?

As I look back over these incredible past 60 years of my

life I can see God's invisible hand guiding and protecting me and putting mentors in my life that provided me with their wisdom. I was born and raised on a dairy farm in Nebraska. I was number 12 of 13 children whose dad was a combat medic in WWII and mother who worked in the U.S. Treasury department during WWII. Looking back, I was blessed with the opportunity to drive tractors at age 10 and trucks at 13 starting to build the same hand-eye motor skills I would need later to fly helicopters and airplanes.

Growing up in a large farm family there are a lot of opportunities to work with dangerous equipment as there were not the safety rules we have today. I only fell off a load of bales once and got run over by the trailer. Lucky for me the ground was soft. My brother Mark, who was two years older than me, was a September baby and I was a late July baby. He turned five after school started and I had just turned five when we started kindergarten and we were in classes with kids who were almost six, from smaller families, who could read already. I bring this up because it affected my primary school years in that I was immature compared to those in my class. It wasn't until I was out of high school that I understood that I wasn't as dumb as I thought I was. I just couldn't catch up and keep up with my classmates. It never dawned on me that my parents had their hands full with 13 kids, when the other kids were probably getting more help at home. My brother and I just kept falling farther behind every year. At the end of my fourth grade and my brother's sixth grade year were both barely making Cs and Ds. The school said we did good enough to pass but my parents finally realized we had fallen way behind so they made arrangements to send us to a different school and repeat fourth and sixth grades. I would love to say that overnight we started to excel in school, but I would be lying. It wasn't until my Dad had died of a heart attack and I was about to start my junior year in high school that I realized that I wasn't as dumb as I thought and I could do well in school and get As and Bs instead of low Bs and Cs. Also at this time one of my older sisters (JoAnne) was an Army helicopter mechanic with plans to go to Army Warrant Officer (WO) pilot training. My brother, David, who was six years older had graduated the AF Academy and was in fixed wing pilot training. I also had 2 brothers-in-law who were Marine and Army Infantry in Vietnam who told me many stories of how WO helo pilots saved the day.

Up to this point I had the chance to get a couple of short Cessna rides and I had marveled as I watched the helicopter and fixed wing crop dusters flying low and fast. I started to want to fly myself. I formulated a plan to do so, and since 9 of my older siblings had served in the military I decided I could join the Army to reach my goal. Since my Dad had passed away at this time a local gun collector, Mr. Woolston, and retired AF Master Sergeant who was my high school Auto mechanics teacher, Mr Goodrich, provided me the mentoring I needed to pursue my dream of flying. Knowing my poor grades would not allow me to get into college or an Academy, I finished my junior year and contacted the local Army recruiter and he set up the ASVAB and FAST(Flight) tests for me to take. I exceeded the ASVAB score to become an officer and scored a 124 on the FAST when only 90 was needed for selection. My recruiter started the paperwork for Warrant Officer Flight Training (WOFT) selection. He also told me that I needed a backup job choice if I wasn't selected for WOFT as a high school student and that the vast majority of WOFT selectees were already in the Army at time of selection.

That summer I traveled to my brother David's Air Force pilot training graduation at Del Rio, TX. I told him and many of his classmates about my flying plans and they were encouraging, but David knowing my poor performance in school cautioned me to not be too optimistic about getting selected or making it through a flight program. In the fall of my senior year we finished all the WOFT selection paperwork and my recruiter submitted it for review. I made a valiant effort to get As and Bs my senior year and in December I received word that I was not selected as a Primary attendee for WOFT but as an alternate. The recruiter said he had no idea if alternates actually got to fill in for someone, so he suggested I enlist in the Army and then reapply on active duty. My spirit was crushed but knew I could still make it happen. In January I enlisted as a helicopter mechanic like my sister JoAnne but with the new Army UH-60 Blackhawk instead of the OH-58. In May I graduated high school with a class rank of 34 out of 36 students.

Three months later my sister JoAnne was starting WOFT at Ft Rucker and I was at Ft Jackson where I breeze through Boot camp and went on to Ft Eustis, VA for UH-60 Crew Chief training. While there I did very well because of all my farm experience and auto mechanics training I had in high school from Mr Goodrich. I was given Ft Campbell, KY for my assignment when I wanted Ft Lewis, WA since my sister Nancy and her Marine Gunny Sgt husband Byron lived just south in Portland, OR. I ended up being able to trade with a classmate who got the only Ft Lewis assignment in our class. While completing UH-60 training at Ft Eustis I decided to update my WOFT package and resubmit. I also mentioned to some of my fellow Army E-1s my desire to be a Warrant Officer and pilot. One of the knuckleheads with his vast 6 months of Army experience looked at me and said, "You're not officer material." I said back, "What does officer material look like," and he pointed to one of the other E-1s who was a bit taller, and I admit much handsomer than I. Later that week while in line at the Personnel office trying to submit my WOFT package, the E-1 sitting next to me asked what I was doing there.

I replied that I was submitting my WOFT package. He looked at me all serious and said, "Oh, don't apply now. I hear there is a 2 year waiting list to go." I said, "Well if I wait 2 years to apply and there is still a 2 year waiting list then I will not start for 4 years. But if I apply now I will only have to wait 2 years and not 4." It was my turn to see the Personnel Sergeant. I handed her my paperwork and she said, "I suggest you wait until you get to Ft Lewis next month and submit it there, because if we take it and need extra material or we lose it, there is not much you can do from 3000 miles away in Washington state." Very good advice I thought and off I went with WOFT package in hand.

I signed into Ft Lewis and got assigned to the newest UH-60 unit, Bravo Company, 9th Combat Aviation Battalion(CAB), (my sister JoAnne had served in Charlie Company, 9th CAB 5 years prior). Most of the Blackhawks had just recently arrived from the Sikorsky factory in Connecticut. On my first day in the unit I was scheduled to get the new guy brief from the company commander. At the end of the briefing the captain asked me if there was anything he could do for me. I said, "I want to apply to WOFT and be a pilot." He said, "Sure, when you get the paperwork all together, I will be more than happy to sign it." I reached into my briefcase and pulled out the WOFT package I completed at Ft Eustis and said, "Here Sir, I have it all done and ready to sign." With a surprised look on his face he took it from my hands, signed it and said, "OK, take it to the Battalion HQ across the street for the Battalion Commander to sign, and have a good day." So off I went, handed it to the Battalion secretary and she made me an appointment to come back in a week to meet the Battalion Commander. After a week of fixing helicopters I reported for my appointment. The BN CO had my paperwork in hand and had me sit down. He told me that he would sign my paperwork but emphasized that he didn't believe I would get selected because I was only a new E-2 and not a sergeant like many of the Battalion's sergeants who had WOFT applications on file. He also reminded me that I didn't have any medals and had no work experience. After he signed it, I said, "I understand and thank you." I drove over to Brigade HQ and turned the paperwork in there. They called me the next day and told me the BDE CO signed it and to come get the paperwork to have it sent to the Selection Board. So in just over a week I had my application all signed and sent off to Department of the Army.

For the next 6 months I became a full-fledged crew chief and was assigned my own Blackhawk to care for and fly missions on. Oct 5th arrived, which was the same day my sister JoAnne was graduating from her WOFT class at Ft Rucker. I got a message while completing a post flight inspection to contact the Ft Lewis Personnel office. (Pre-cell phone days) I go to our tool room and call the number. A lady answered and told me that I had been selected for WOFT and had to report to Ft Rucker for class in 10 days. I asked, "How many days do I get to drive there?" She said, "Eight." I then asked, "How many days does it take to out-process from Ft Lewis?" She said, "Normally five, so you better get on it." I immediately informed my supervisor and he told me I had better hurry up and get out of here and get to Ft Rucker. The whole Battalion was shocked that this new E-3 was on his way to WOFT when several sergeants had not been selected. I called JoAnne to congratulate her on her graduation and gave her my news, to which she said, "Do you want to buy my car I have here so I don't have to drive it home?" I told her yes and was able to get out of Ft Lewis in a record 2 days and made it to Ft Rucker by the end of the 10th day.

My Class 84-11 was filled with men of all ages, ranks, and career fields. I was blessed to be surrounded with warriors 5-15 years older than me. We had tank drivers, Rangers,

Special Forces, and several other helicopter crew chiefs all wanting to be Army aviators. During the next year, I was trained and mentored by Vietnam veterans in an effort to make me a combat aviator. I excelled in the cockpit and in academics and battled back and forth for the #1 and #2 spot, but as a less than mature 20 year old compared to 27 year old sergeants, my officership was near the bottom of the class. Because I could run a 10 minute 2-mile and max the PT test, the Instructors cut me some slack in the officership training. I was second in the class to solo the TH-55, the only one to get to fly solo in the OH-58, and first one to complete night vision goggle (NVG) qualification. A couple of weeks prior to follow-on aircraft selection I called my brother David who was flying the AF A-10 and told him I would be able to pick any aircraft and was leaning towards the UH-60 since I know so much about it. He told me I would enjoy the AH-1 Cobra Attack Helicopter better. So that is what I chose on assignment night.

During the final few months of flight training many of the Instructors advised me to go to Korea for my first AH-1 assignment. They said the flying would be fun, I would be in a constant state of war preparedness, and because of the high turnover of pilots due to the one year assignment I would upgrade to Pilot-in-Command (PIC) in six months as opposed to 18-24 months everywhere else. They also said that Delta Troop 4/7th Air Cavalry Squadron was the best unit to get assigned to in Korea. I finished WOFT and AH-1 qualification and on 2 January 1985, I reported to Young Sung Barracks for placement into a flying unit. Only by God's grace was I assigned to Delta Troop and was put on a bus towards the DMZ for Camp LaGuardia, an airfield within artillery range of North Korea.

For the next year I was blessed to be surrounded by Vietnam veterans like CW4 Ed Kenney and CW2 Jeff

Coate who not only taught me how to fly the Cobra to its limits in preparation for combat with North Korea, but they mentored me as an officer to help me become as good a Warrant Officer and pilot as I could be. They also encouraged all us new pilots to use our off-duty time wisely and had me doing Korean martial arts five nights a week. I was able to test for my 1st Degree Black belt in Hap-Kido and fight in an amateur kick boxing contest. Since Camp LaGuardia was one mile from Camp Red Cloud (CRC), which was a much larger compound with a library and testing center, I was about to walk there during my lunch break throughout the year to take CLEP tests. I decided since the CLEP tests were free I would take as many as I could and if I passed them I would receive free college credit. I ended up receiving 46 college credits through CLEP for my efforts. As for the flying, it was OUTSTANDING. And as advertised, Ed Kenney signed me off as PIC in six months. During the next 6 months I flew a lot of demanding NVG missions, patrolled the DMZ, and helped train the pilots replacing me. One quote Jeff Coate said that has always guided me during my next 28 years of military service. Jeff said, "When you stop having fun and enjoying your job, you need to quit and do something else."

When I had 3 months left in Korea I had to apply for a follow on assignment. I asked to go to Ft Bragg, NC the home of the 82nd Airborne Division, but I also asked to stay in Korea an extra 6 months before going to Ft Bragg. To everyone's surprise the Army turned down my extension request, but did assign me to Ft Bragg to report 2 Jan 1986.

I departed Korea on 19 Dec 1985, went to Nebraska for Christmas and reported to Ft Bragg, NC on 6 January 1986. I was blessed to be assigned to Bravo Company, 82nd Attack Helicopter Battalion, where I meet the BEST Commander I had in my 30 year career.

Captain Greg Williamitis was a warrior with a desire to push his pilots to their full potential in and out of the cockpit. When I met him I asked him if I could be authorized to take college night classes with Embry-Riddle(ERAU) on base, he said, "You can take as many classes as you want, but I expect you to train hard and carry your share of the load if not more. Oh yeah, also I want all my pilots to attend Jump School at Ft Benning." That afternoon I drove to the ERAU office handed them my 46 CLEP credits of which they credited 39 towards my BS degree and they told me they would give me 45 credits for my flight experience. This left me with having to earn 42 credits (14 classes) through night school. Since not all required classes were taught each 8 week semester, we laid out a course load to finish my BS degree in 1 year. Their semesters were 8 weeks long, classes were held M-F evenings from 6-8 and 8-10 and all day on Saturdays. So you could knock out 15 semester hours every 8 weeks if you didn't have any responsibility and wanted to kill yourself. From January – July I knocked out as many classes as I could while flying a demanding schedule. In June Captain Williamitis asked me when I planned to go to Jump School. I told him I could go at the end of August when July classes were over. He scheduled me for a late August class at Ft Benning and since I didn't have night classes for two weeks in August I had some free time to have a social life. On August 1st, I met my future wife Pam, and for the record, we got engaged less than 2 months later and married six months later. We have been married for almost 36 years. I think sometimes she wishes I would have not taken a break from night classes. From late Sept 1986 to the first week of March 1987 I finished up my BS degree from ERAU.

Once I had my degree I called Army personnel center in DC and asked if I could get out of the Army a year earlier than my current commitment to go to the Air Force/Navy/Marines. They kind of laughed and said, "NO, we have a shortage of AH-1 pilots and you aren't even close to the other services pilot training age limit." I contacted the other service recruiters and asked what their requirements were for applying for fixed wing pilot training. The Marines told me I had to be completely out of the Army before I could apply. The Air Force and Navy told me that when I was within 1 year of my date of separation (DOS) I could apply. I really wanted to fly the AV-8 Harrier but now with a wife and a child on the way I could not go without a job waiting to find out if I was selected. Having marked off the Marines, I signed up and took the AFOQT and Navy Officer/Flight tests. I maxed both tests and on 20 September 1987 submitted my applications to the AF and Navy for OTS/OCS and pilot training. Also during this summer my Attack Battalion was selecting pilots to transition to the new AH-64 Apache. Captain Williamitis called me into his office and said I was at the top of his list for the Apache, but that he had heard a rumor I was planning to get out of the Army. Since I respected him so much it was the hardest thing I had do to tell him that I wanted to fly jets in the AF or Navy and couldn't accept another 3 year commitment for the Apache. He said that was fine and wished me the best of luck. In September 1987 after we flew the Cobras to the boneyard, I moved across the airfield to Charlie Troop 1/17 Air Cavalry where I finished out my time in the Army training new pilots in combat tactics.

January of 1988 was the start of a busy year. In mid-January I was hired by North and South Carolina Army Guard units to fly AH-64s, Maryland Highway Patrol for Air Medivac, and I was selected by both the AF and Navy for Pilot training. Since the AF informed me one week prior to the Navy, I chose the AF. Pam and I had our first son Daniel in April and I was busy flying and deploying right up to my DOS of 19 September. On 1 October I reported to AF OTS and learned very quickly the AF didn't care that I could max a PT test or run a sub-

5 minute mile. As opposed to the Army's 70% passing score, the AF demanded a minimum of 85% and they expected me to be able to write reports and papers and use IS, ARE, WAS, WERE, BE, BEING, and BEEN properly in sentences. At the end of my first week I called home and told Pam I was going to flunk out of OTS. My class was filled with guys who had REAL Engineering Degrees and some had been Engineers for NASA, and could actually write papers the way the AF wanted them written and not with crayons like Army grunts. She assured me all I needed to do was buckle down, work hard, and find some help. I was blessed to have a great teacher in my flight that got me through the writing portions. I ended up not getting less than a 95% on all my tests and I was able to help my classmates with Officer/Leadership training and physical fitness.

In January 1989, I was commissioned a 2Lt and was off to Vance AFB, OK. I collected my wife and 9 month old son and started AF UPT to learn to fly fast and hopefully get a fighter aircraft at graduation. Upon arriving at Vance AFB and seeing the T-37s/T-38s flying I remembered my brother David telling me that anyone can fly a helicopter but jet training is much harder. So for the next year I worked hard and tried my best to help the other students in my class understand radio calls, IFR flight, navigation, and formation flight. I was blessed with a great T-37 Instructor, Captain Greer, whom we called "Daddy Rabbit." He had flown the B-52. Once we mastered the "Mighty Tweet" it was on to the T-38 to learn how to fly and land much faster. My brother was right in that the T-38 take-off speed was faster than max speed of the AH-1. But the runway was two miles long and you didn't have to fly in between trees, so it was much safer. As we approached graduation I called my brother David again and said, "With all my Army experience I think I want to fly the OV-10 or A-10 since the FAC/CAS mission for the Army is their primary mission." David told me to ask for an F-16 so I could get some fast jet experience and then if I became a FAC later on in my career I would have both Army and F-16 CAS experience. So I asked for an F-16 as my first choice and got it on assignment night. I received the Commander's trophy at UPT graduation, packed up Pam and Daniel and was off to Fighter Lead-In Training in New Mexico where we were taught the basics of aerial combat and dropping bombs in modified T-38. This allowed us to quickly learn new skills in a jet we were familiar with and it was way less expensive to operate than a front line fighter.

In May we arrived at MacDill AFB to learn how to fly the F-16C Fighting Falcon (better known as the Viper or Lawn Dart.) I kid you not, but it seemed 1 out of every 3 instructor pilots had ejected from an F-16. Having flown a single-engine helicopter at night under NVGs in the trees, knowing you were going to die every time you flew, I quickly fell in love with the Viper and its powerful engine, awesome flight characteristics, and great ejection seat. Flying the F-16 was a lot like flying the AH-1 from the front seat with the sidestick controls and excellent field of view. Upon completion of both air-to-air and air-to-ground phases of training we prepared to move to Homestead AFB, FL. Prior to moving, my second son Andrew was born just as Desert Shield kicked off and we all thought we would be sent right over to the Middle East. But it was all over before we knew it.

While at Homestead AFB, I was blessed with the opportunity to fly the newest F-16C Block 40s brand new from the factory. I had great commanders, awesome training missions, and outstanding TDYs to Norway and Las Vegas to test our combat skills. Getting to fly the F-16 alongside some hard charging fighter pilots was a dream come true and every time I flew the Viper I marveled that I had been allowed the opportunity to do so. I remember many times looking out the canopy at my wingman and thinking, am I really doing this? I barely graduated high school, and now I am flying a multi-million dollar frontline fighter. Only by God's grace and only in America. My time of living the dream came to a halt due to Hurricane Andrew destroying the base and surrounding area. Just prior to the Hurricane I had been told to be prepared for new assignment to Korea with the F-16 or an Air Liaison Officer (ALO/FAC) tour at an Army base.

When Hurricane Andrew hit I decided that since we had just lost everything we owned that taking an assignment to Korea was not a good idea so I decided to take the ALO/FAC job at Ft Bragg that allowed my family to be close to relatives as we rebuilt our lives. Since I was already Parachute/Airborne qualified and had been in the 82nd Airborne before, I was put right to work with the Aviation Brigade. A few months after arriving at Ft Bragg for the second time, our third son Turner was born.

My brother David had been right many years earlier. Prior Army experience combined with CAS experience in the F-16 allowed me to excel as an ALO/FAC. We were a young group of captains doing major's jobs because not too many AF majors were dumb enough to want to parachute out of a "perfectly good" airplane. My commanders were awesome and allowed us to come up with innovative ways to train. The enlisted troops were also super motivated. I had tons of opportunities to do many things 99% of AF officers never get to do: 110 parachute jumps, working with Army Infantry, Aviation, Special Forces, Marines, and Navy SEALS. I worked routinely with JSOC on some very cool missions, even getting to run a 4 day CALFEX to demonstrate SOF operations for US Congressmen and the President and Vice President. The last major operation I took part in was "Operation Uphold Democracy," where I was tapped to be the lead AF officer for the Airborne invasion of Haiti. I learned more in the lead up to that operation than I had the previous year. As my tour started to wind down I was up for a new assignment and since I was a Jump ALO I got any assignment I wanted. Pam and I chose to go RAF Lakenheath England where I would get to fly the F-15E Strike Eagle.

After a few months of F-15E training at Seymour-Johnson AFB, we crossed the ocean for our new home at RAF Lakenheath. The Strike Eagle was definitely a go-to-war fighter with powerful engines, lots of gas, and could carry a wide variety of weapons and lots of them. Again, the aircrew I had the privilege to fly and work with were outstanding and motivated. Flying in Europe and two deployments to enforce the No-Fly Zone in Northern Iraq was demanding but very exciting. I was constantly amazed that I had the privilege to fly this expensive fighter and lead packages of 30+ aircraft over Northern Iraq. All of the pilots and WSOs I worked with had outstanding backgrounds and many went on to Test Pilot School and Weapons School. I sometimes felt like an imposter not having a Masters in Aerodynamics from MIT or even an Engineering degree at all. The brain power in the mission planning room was always humbling and sometimes I jokingly wondered if the wing leadership would find out I didn't belong and have me arrested for impersonating an officer and pilot.

Up to this point in my career not only was there very little talk about becoming an airline pilots among all the aircrew I worked with, but I was still under the impression that mostly cargo pilots had the qualifications to fly for the airlines. Near the end of our tour an F-15C pilot moved down the street from me. This guy had flown for American Airlines but was furloughed a couple years before and came back on active duty to wait it out. After a few Saturday afternoons talking with him, his enthusiasm for the airline pilot life made an impression on me. I finished out my tour in the F-15E and decided to return to Air Training Command to instruct in the venerable T-37 Tweet primary trainer. Again like the ALO/FAC assignment it was not one many fighter pilots chose to take. But for me, I remembered back to my mentors in helicopters telling me that before I retire from the military I needed to help train the next generation to be ready to replace me and my peers. Also, I felt that instructing brand new student pilots how to fly would be more fun and challenging than teaching in the T-38 where students already know how to fly and are just being taught how to fly faster.

I headed to Randolph AFB, TX for the 3-month long T-37 Pilot Instructor Training (PIT) and proficiency advanced through the training in just over a month. I arrived at Columbus AFB, two months early and jumped right into teaching the basics of military flying: contact, acrobatics, spins, instruments, and formation. After 3 months I was giving my own flight of instructors and a class of students to lead and assist in becoming the best pilots they could be. In the middle of my second student class I was asked to be Chief of T-37 Standards for the Wing. This was an awesome job in that I had the opportunity to fly with the entire Wing's T-37 Instructors and students and not just those of a single flight. About this same time I went on a weekend student cross country flight with a student whose dad was a Southwest Airlines Captain. We flew to Houston where between training flights I had the wonderful opportunity to learn about the airline business and specifically that Southwest was an awesome place to work and was growing rapidly. After this weekend I started to listen and take notes as many other instructors on base talked about airline requirements and application processes. I also found out that I could use my GI-Bill to pay for a portion of a Boeing 737 Type rating that would be required to work for Southwest.

With only two years left before I could retire, I attended a 737 Type rating class with Higher Power Aviation in Dallas, TX where for the first time I learned what it would be like to fly a large aircraft with more than two flap settings (up and down). At this same time I was asked to be part of the initial cadre for the new AF T-6A Texan II and help start a new Primary Pilot training unit at Moody AFB, GA. I jumped on the chance to fly this awesome new plane and help mold it and Instructors to provide 21st century training. With my prior maintenance experience I took on the Functional Check Flight (FCF) roll and got to mold the process for this new aircraft in relation to keeping them fixed and flying. While at Moody AFB, I applied to Southwest Airlines on 1 September 2001. But because of the tragedy on 9/11, it wasn't until December that I received a call from Southwest for an interview in January 2002. In February I received the wonderful news that I had been hired and the waiting game began. It wasn't until March 2004 that I actually started training with Southwest, so during that 2 year wait, I was in the hired pool waiting for my turn to start. During the first year of the wait I was still on active duty where I continued to teach in the T-6 and I deployed to Kuwait to help advise the US Army commanders during their preparations for the Invasion of Iraq. During my second year I taught math at a middle school, worked in Saudi Arabia for my brother Mark teaching F-15S classes to Saudi trainees, and I worked as a security guard for Walmart. I had several job offers to fly for some corporate flight departments but I knew that I would leave as soon as I got the call from Southwest for a training class and I didn't want these companies to spend the money to train me and then I leave. But I am here to tell you that the two year wait for a Southwest employee number was well worth it. 19 years of flying almost a 1,000 hours a year at Southwest and becoming a Captain at a major airline was a dream that I thought I would never be able to accomplish or even be given the opportunity.

As I look back 40+ years, had my parents not held me back in the fourth grade, I would have fallen farther behind my peers. If I had gone right to WOFT out of high school, I believe I would have graduated but I would have been an immature officer and not have the maintenance background that paid dividends all these years. If I had gone to Ft Campbell vs Ft Lewis it would have put me a year behind because their policy was a year on station before being able to applying for WOFT vs immediately like I benefited from at Ft Lewis. If I had stayed at Ft Lewis a few more months I might have been killed in the Blackhawk I had been assigned as a crew chief, as it crashed soon after I got to Ft Rucker. If I had taken a UH-60 vs the AH-1 out of WOFT, I would have been stationed in Panama where there was less opportunity to take college classes. If the Army had not denied my Korea extension, I might not have met my wife. Having been a helicopter pilot allowed me to excel in AF pilot training and gave me a unique perspective while flying fighters, being an ALO/FAC, and leading warriors into combat zones. As I look back I can see how God orchestrated each event in my life and career that allowed me to build upon each major experience to make me a better officer, pilot, leader, and instructor. I have had an unorthodox and unusual flying career that has not only been challenging, but has been very fun and rewarding. After reading the book "Outliers" I wholeheartedly agree with the author in his observations and I recommend to anyone that when given an opportunity to do something few others are doing, jump on the opportunity (as long as it is legal and moral). Never take NO for an answer and remember that you have a 100% chance of failure if you don't start. There is no cookie cutter approach to any career and if you take opportunities presented to you and work hard you can achieve the impossible. Some people might say I am just lucky. But as my high school wrestling coach used to say: "Luck is when Preparation meets Opportunity."

Tell us about the different ministries you've supported

I will start with what I believe God calls us to do and that is to support His Church and the ministers who proclaim the Gospel. So, Pam and I have tithed to the churches we have belonged to and continue to do so. This allows the local church to provide assistance to those in the community and missions around the world. We support Lottie Moon International Missions and Annie Armstrong Stateside Missions, and Missions in Northern India, Moldova, and a church in Brooklyn NY.

Growing up in a large Pro-Life family (13 brothers and sisters and 80 cousins) being Pro-Life totally makes sense and because we believe "Life" begins at conception, we support both the National Right to Life and the North Carolina Right to Life organizations. We also support the local Pregnancy Care Center that helps women Chose Life and support them throughout their pregnancies. We do this in several ways, one being that I drive the Medical Van one day a week and another is that Pam is an advocate and mentor one day week.

Right now the biggest ministry outside of church I'm involved in is a Post-Prison ministry called Redemption Place. With the help of Turner, we oversee the 501c3 portion of Redemption Place and with coordination with our rental company, Opieland Rentals, we provide 8 acres of land, a pond, and 3 houses that allow Redemption Place to provide high quality housing for Former prisoners to live and go through a one-year program to get reintegrated back into society. Redemption Place also assists these men get their drivers licenses, get a car, learn how to tithe to their church, and save money in a savings account weekly.

I am also part of an organization called Go-Global Ministries. It started as Global Youth Baseball and still uses sports (baseball, soccer and basketball) to spread the Gospel in several counties around the world. I have primarily dealt with the Cuban missions in Northeastern Havana. We partner with a group of 100+ house churches and have assisted in shipping two 40' containers of appliances and sports gear for use in those churches and for youth sports ministries programs.

I am the primary partner in our rental company called Opieland Rentals and Properties. We own 11 houses and use them as a ministry also by providing very nice homes at rental prices that allow people who normally couldn't afford a house in a very good neighborhood to rent a high quality house from a company that makes sure everything works and quickly repairs anything that needs fixed. We also work with our renters in tough times to help them get through it without worrying about getting booted from their home or a big fee imposed.

What are your favorite quotes and sayings?

Over the past 60 years I have heard and use many quotes and sayings and below are some of the ones I like the best.

When things start to get messed up because of the fast paced life I live: "Life in the Fast Lane, check it and see, Got a fever of 103, come on baby you can do more than dance, Life in the Fast Lane." It is two 1970's songs mixed together.

Military and work settings:

1. In the Air Force, leadership espoused "Flexibility is the keyto Air Power." Captain Glen "Six Packi" Ribikie's add on to that quote was: "Flexibility is the Key to Air Power, Poor Planning is the Key to Flexibility."

2. "To err is human, to really foul things up requires acomputer." Mr. Fraizer, HS math teacher

3. "All leave is canceled until moral gets better."

4. "The only reward for hard work is NO punishment."

5. "A computer makes as many mistakes in two seconds as 20 men working 20 years make."

6. The Soviet military used to say "War is chaos, theAmerican military practices chaos everyday, that is why they do so well in War."

I believe in getting tasks done immediately so I have several sayings for that and many come from the book "The One Minute Manager":

1. "If it only takes 2 minutes to get it done, do it now."

2. "If you spent half as much time doing something right asyou do trying to avoid doing it, it would be done already."

3. "Why do most business opportunities fail: Because theydon't get started." Overcoming the inertia of starting anything is the hardest part, once you learn how to overcome that inertia you can start many projects.

4. "Don't give me 10 reasons why not to do something, giveme 1 reason to do it that is moral and legal and do it."

5. "People who say things can't be done are usuallyinterrupted by people doing them."

Now, on the funny side of trying to get people and my kids inspired to do things, I love using many things found in "Dis-Insperational" quotes:

1. "Winners never quit, Quitters never win, but those whonever win and never quit are just plain dumb."

2. "There is a Silver lining in every cloud, but thousands ofpeople are struck dead by lighting every year trying to find it."

3. "Never underestimate the power of stupid people in a largegroup."

4. "Maybe the only reason for your miserable life is to be awarning to others."

5. "Put off until tomorrow what you don't want to do today."

6. "Hard work often pays off over time, but Laziness alwayspays off NOW."

7. "Maybe that light at the end of the tunnel is a Freight Train."

In the area of finances and business, and some sayings that come from "Rich Dad, Poor Dad".

1. "It doesn't matter how much you make, it's how much youspend."

2. "It doesn't matter how much you make, it's how much youcan keep from the government."

3. "All my rich friends have lost a lot of money, but all mypoor friends haven't lost a dime."

4. "Money can't buy you happiness, but it sure can makeyour life easier."

I love quoting Murphy's Laws, some are for the military and some are for all occasions.

Murphy's general laws

1. Nothing is as easy as it looks.

2. Everything takes longer than you think.

3. Anything that can go wrong will go wrong, and it willhappen at the worst time.

4. If there is a possibility of several things going wrong, theone that will cause the most damage will be the one to go wrong.

5. Left to themselves, things tend to go from bad to worse.

6. If everything seems to be going well, you have obviouslyoverlooked something.

7. Nature always sides with the hidden flaw.

8. It is impossible to make anything foolproof because foolsare so ingenious.

9. Whenever you set out to do something, something elsemust be done first.

10. Life is tough, then you die.

Murphy's Military Laws of Armed conflict

1. If the enemy is in range, so are you.

2. Incoming fire has the right of way.

3. Don't look conspicuous, it draws fire.

4. There is always a way.

5. The easy way is always mined.

6. Try to look unimportant, they may be low on ammo.

7. Professionals are predictable, it's the amateurs that aredangerous and the world is full of amateurs.

8. The enemy invariably attacks on two occasions:

    a. When you're ready for them.

    b. When you're not ready for them.

9. Teamwork is essential, it gives them someone else to shootat.

10. If you can't remember, the claymore is pointed at you.

11. The enemy diversion you have been ignoring will be themain attack.

12. A "sucking chest wound" is natures way of telling you toslow down.

13. If your attack is going well, you have walked into anambush.

14. Never draw fire, it irritates everyone around you.

15. Anything you do can get you shot, including nothing.

16. Make it tough enough for the enemy to get in and youwon't be able to get out.

17. Never share a foxhole with anyone braver than yourself.

18. If you are short of everything but the enemy, you are in acombat zone.

19. When you have secured an area, don't forget to tell theenemy.

20. Never forget that your weapon is made by the lowestbidder.

21. Friendly Fire Isn't.

22. The only thing more accurate than enemy fire, is FriendlyFire.

23. Whenever you need two items to be put together to makesomething function, they are never shipped together nor at the same time.

Explanation of the book title and Final thoughts now that you turned 60?

⋯⋯⋯⋯⋯⋯⋯ ❦❦ ⋯⋯⋯⋯⋯⋯⋯

Wow, what a journey God has guided and protected me throughout these past 60 years. I have done many "Dangerous" things and like the song in Top Gun I have constantly lived and operated in the "The Danger Zone".

The Duct Tape reference is to the fact that Duct Tape (or in aviation speak 100 mile per hour tape) is a staple in my life. I grew up on a farm where we had to do most of the fixing of our equipment. Most of the time if something was broke we either cut it off with a torch or welded it back together or duct taped it in place until we got it home. I am not a perfectionist and I am what some call an 80% type of guy. My understanding in most situations the effort to take a project from 80% to 100% perfect requires twice the effort it took to get the project start to 80%.

Most people people who know me well know I am a master of the use of Duct Tape and always have some handy to fix things to the 80% level and get things rolling.

When I was 21 the mentors I flew with were 35 and had fought in Vietnam and I just thought they were Old and had lots of wisdom. But when I got to 35 myself with a wife and 3 sons, I understood that 'Looking like you were wise, and being wise were not the same.'

Some people say time flys by fast and flys faster as you get older. I don't believe that, nor feel that way. I believe filling every available moment with trying to be the hands and feet of Jesus here on Earth helps the days, hours, minutes be as God planned them. With relationships with family and friends and trying to raise children to follow God, time doesn't seem to me to move very fast as I have enjoyed almost every minute of it.

Someone might read these 68 "Chapters" or "Answers to questions" and think that I didn't realize until I was turning 60 how blessed my life has been. I want everyone who reads this to know I give credit to God and my Lord and Savior Jesus Christ for the wonderfully awesome life I have been privileged to live. I have known for most of my adult life that I was blessed with a wonderful and beautiful wife and children whom I thank God everyday for allowing me to be their father. I truly understand the blessings of each of our awesome grand children.

My wish for my sons is that they continue to trust God in their everyday lives, that they continue to be the wonderful husbands, fathers, and sons that they are and that they give thanks to God for the blessings of their families God has granted them.

I pray that our grandchildren continue to grow in their faith and trust in their Lord and Savior Jesus Christ and that they look for ways to serve Him by serving others.

I hope that for the rest of my life with Pam that I will be as good as a husband as she deserves and that God calls me to be.

Having survived growing up on a farm with a family of 13 kids and lots of animals and farm equipment. Then living through all the dangerous stuff I did all while being married to a wonderful wife and helping raise God fearing children has allowed me to have a prospective on life that I hope many who read this book can have also.

My final thought for these chapters are "Without Faith in God and Jesus Christ" life would be hard to bare, and my prayer for everyone is that they seek the Creator of Life and trust him with your life. When you meet the future spouse God puts in your life, don't wait until you can "Afford to get married or ready to be married" because you will never really reach either of those goals and you will have a lot of wasted years waiting. Also, don't "Wait" to have children until you are "ready or can afford them," because you will never be ready nor be able to "afford" them and again waste many years waiting to meet those requirements.

www.ingramcontent.com/pod-product-compliance
Lightning Source LLC
Chambersburg PA
CBHW051258120626
46547CB00015B/1990